Postmodernism has evoked great controversy and continues to do so today, especially now that it is disseminating into general discourse. Some see its principles, such as its fundamental resistance to metanarratives, as frighteningly disruptive, but a growing number are reaping the benefits of its innovative perspective. In *Political Theory and Postmodernism*, Stephen K. White outlines a path through the postmodern problematic by distinguishing two distinct ways of thinking about the meaning of responsibility, one prevalent in modern and the other in postmodern perspectives. Using this as a guide, White explores the work of Heidegger, Foucault, Derrida, Lyotard, and Habermas, as well as that of "difference" feminists, with the goal of showing how postmodernism can inform contemporary ethical–political reflection.

Postmodernism's well-known stances of resistance and impertinence must be supplemented, he argues, by a more affirmative orientation to "otherness," taking the form of a certain "lightness of care" that emerges from cultivating an ambivalent mood in which grief at the loss of certainties and delight in difference are inseparably intertwined. In his concluding chapter, White examines how this revised postmodern perspective might bear on our thinking about justice.

POLITICAL THEORY AND POSTMODERNISM

MODERN EUROPEAN PHILOSOPHY

Executive editor

RAYMOND GEUSS, COLUMBIA UNIVERSITY

Editorial board

HIDE ISHIGURO, KEIO UNIVERSITY, JAPAN
ALAN MONTEFIORE, BALLIOL COLLEGE, OXFORD
MARY TILES, UNIVERSITY OF HAWAII

POLITICAL THEORY AND POSTMODERNISM

STEPHEN K. WHITE

*Virginia Polytechnic Institute
and State University*

CAMBRIDGE
UNIVERSITY PRESS

Published by the Press Syndicate of the University of Cambridge
The Pitt Building, Trumpington Street, Cambridge CB2 1RP
40 West 20th Street, New York, NY 10011-4211, USA
10 Stamford Road, Oakleigh, Victoria 3166, Australia

First published 1991
Reprinted 1992

Printed in Canada

Library of Congress Cataloging-in-Publication Data
White, Stephen K.
Political theory and postmodernism / Stephen K. White.
p.   cm. – (Modern European philosophy)
Includes bibliographical references and index.
ISBN 0-521-40122-4. – ISBN 0-521-40948-9 (pbk.)
1. Political science – Philosophy.   2. Political ethics.
3. Postmodernism.   I. Title.   II. Series.
JA71.W456   1991   91-9374
                                                            CIP

British Library Cataloguing in Publication Data
White, Stephen K.
Political theory and postmodernism. – (Modern European
philosophy).
1. Philosophy. Postmodernism
I. Title   II. Series
190

ISBN 0-521-40122-4 hardback
ISBN 0-521-40948-9 paperback

To
LYDIA

CONTENTS

PREFACE

The term "postmodernism" is one that elicits both enthusiasm and distrust. The former results from the polysemic implications of being liberated from the dogmas of modernity; the latter from concern about the ways in which postmodern modes of thinking sometimes seem to revel in a refusal to engage problems central to any continuity of modern discourse. This tension is compounded by conceptual complexities surrounding the notion of postmodernity. For example, it seems to stretch in unclear ways, from art, architecture, and literature to philosophy, social theory, and politics; and it is associated with other hotly contested concepts, such as "post-structuralism." I attempt to chart a course into this field of tension, with the primary intention of illuminating ethical and political questions.

I begin by laying out what, from my perspective, are the essential postmodern issues that contemporary ethical–political reflection needs to address. I refer in the Introduction to a "postmodern problematic," constituted by four phenomena: growing incredulity toward traditional metanarratives, new awareness of the costs of societal rationalization, the explosion of informational technologies, and the emergence of new social movements. The elucidation of this problematic, however, merely provides one with some prominent landmarks. It does not yet tell one how to travel, or, rather, how to think through the problematic. That answer begins to emerge in Chapter 2, where some distinctions are offered that help one understand why a peculiar repetitiveness is evident in the battles that swirl around postmodernism. These distinctions are initially elaborated in the context of specific controversies between some of the main participants in these struggles, especially Jürgen Habermas, on the one hand, and Michel Foucault, Jacques Derrida, and Jean-François Lyotard, on the other. In regard to what animates the basic reflections – moral, political, aesthetic – of each side, I distinguish between a sense of "responsibility to act" and a sense of "responsibility to otherness." Corresponding to this distinction is one relating to language: its "action-coordinating" function and its "world-disclosing" function. Understanding these distinctions, as well as why they are viewed differently by the two sides, is the key to seeing what is at stake in the debates over modernity and postmodernity.

Already at this point, I suspect that a strong defender of postmodernism would be in the throes of Nietzschean laughter. He or she would immediately draw attention to the irony of starting a book about postmodernism with the assertion that everything can be cleared up with the help of a couple of metaphysical–ontological-sounding binary distinctions. However, my use of these two sets of binary distinctions does not imply any strong metaphysical or ontological claims. These distinctions are simply the most basic terms of my scheme for interpreting some of our present dilemmas ("our" refers here primarily to liberal, highly industrialized Western societies). The "validity" of these distinctions is shown only to the degree that they help us address the frustrations and dissatisfactions of modern life, while at the same time doing at least some justice to the traditions and modes of reason that are embedded in that life.

The wrong way to think through the postmodern problematic is to essentialize one side of these distinctions at the expense of the other. And it is just such a strategy that characterizes most positions in the debates over postmodernity. All of my efforts in this book are directed toward finding ways of thinking and acting that keep the two senses of responsibility and the two understandings of language in fruitful tension, allowing neither pair to dictate terms to the other.[1]

The sense of responsibility to act and the understanding of language as a medium for the coordination of action are part of the deep structure of modern Western styles of thinking about ethics and politics. The contrasting pair of concepts constitutes a challenge to this orientation. In Chapters 3 and 4, I argue that it is in Martin Heidegger's work that one finds the most perceptive initial statement of this challenge. In elucidating this work's implications, I pay attention not only to the continuities with current postmodern positions but also to discontinuities. In particular, I argue that in Heidegger's later work there are insights about otherness that have not always been adequately remembered by contemporary postmodernists. At the same time, however, Heidegger leaves us with a perspective on politics and ethics that is at best opaque and at worst disastrous. Heidegger's legacy, then, is one of extraordinary insights into the responsibility to otherness, matched by deeply flawed insights into the responsibility to act. Chapter 5 looks more directly at some contemporary postmodern thinkers, concentrating on this question of how their conceptualizations of responding to otherness might reorient ethical–political action. The exploration here leads to the suggestion that the notion of a certain "lightness" of care for others offers some basis for such a reorientation. In Chapter 6, I turn to "difference" feminism's analysis of care and the fostering of otherness for help in correcting and further developing the insights I draw out of Heidegger and the postmoderns.

The speculation about new practical orientations that is begun

---

1 There *may be* some overlap between the sort of tension I want to argue for and that proposed by Richard Rorty. Our "final vocabulary," he writes, should not provide us with a unifying cement but rather should reflect a tension between "one's sense of obligation" in interaction and one's "ways of dealing with finitude." (The way in which I see finitude being involved in the sense of responsibility toward otherness becomes clear in Chapter 4.) Rorty's thinking about this distinction is quite interesting, but the way it is related to ethical–political issues is unenlightening. All these issues are laid to rest by simply mapping the distinction onto another, naively deployed distinction between the public and private spheres. Our bifurcated vocabulary then fits unproblematically into two airtight boxes. This arrangement yields no difficult questions for public life; and it is precisely such questions that I want to explore. See Rorty, *Contingency, Irony and Solidarity* (Cambridge: Cambridge University Press, 1989), especially pp. 68–9.

in Chapters 5 and 6 becomes more focused in Chapter 7. At issue there is a reconceptualization of justice. The underlying intention is to illustrate the kinds of guidelines one must use in rethinking basic concepts in light of the postmodern problematic. To the degree that my analysis of justice is plausible, others should be encouraged to undertake similar efforts with regard to other concepts.

A few words are in order about what this book is not. It is not intended to be a survey of all the themes that have emerged in discussions about postmodernism. That would require a big book; this is a small one with a specific thesis. Nor does it cover all the philosophers and social theorists who are associated with postmodernism. The omission of thinkers like Jean Baudrillard, however, is not meant to imply that their thought has nothing to say to us about cultural, social, or political analysis.[2] It is a result simply of my judgment that they do not wrestle in quite as sustained a fashion with the ethical–political themes highlighted in these pages as do Foucault, Derrida, and Lyotard. Finally, this is not a book that will flesh out an elaborate picture of what a politics more sensitive to postmodern concerns might look like. Although I do speculate about this in the last chapter, my primary task is to make the case for a partial displacement of the ways we traditionally come at ethical–political reflection. If this effort is successful, the next step is to look more concretely at what this different perspective might imply in terms of altering the shape of specific political processes and institutions.

2 Some of the implications of Baudrillard's work are explored in Timothy W. Luke, *Screens of Power: Ideology, Domination and Resistance in Informational Society* (Urbana: University of Illinois Press, 1989), and Douglas Kellner, *Jean Baudrillard: From Marxism to Postmodernism and Beyond* (Cambridge: Polity Press, 1988).

ACKNOWLEDGMENTS

This book grew out of my dissatisfaction with the way postmoderns and their critics have engaged one another. My search for a better way to think about this engagement was supported initially by the Center for Programs in the Humanities at Virginia Polytechnic Institute and State University. The generous support of the Alexander von Humboldt Foundation allowed me to spend the 1987–8 academic year at the University of Frankfurt, where I finally came to an understanding with Heidegger. I would particularly like to thank Jürgen Habermas for his hospitality there, especially given his deep reservations about my project. The Alexander von Humboldt organization also deserves extraordinary thanks. It is perhaps as close to the Platonic form of a foundation as an academic is likely to find. A number of people in Frankfurt contributed to the evolution of my ideas during that year, including Richard Bernstein, Alessandro Ferrara, Rainer Forst, Chris Latiolais, and Richard Wolin.

In the spring of 1989, the Humboldt Foundation was generous enough to invite me back to Germany, to a conference on Heidegger in Bonn. The paper presented there helped me formulate some of the ideas in Chapters 3 and 4. Near the completion of the manuscript in spring 1990, I presented a paper on "The Critical Theory/Postmodernism Controversy" to the interdisciplinary graduate program in Methodologies for the Study of Western History and Culture at Trent University. This was most helpful in the final refinement of my overall perspective, and I thank Douglas Torgerson and Robert Carter for that opportunity.

People who were generous enough to read and criticize various chapters include Tom Dumm, Bonnie Honig, Axel Honneth, and Dennis Schmidt. The last of these helped immensely at the very beginning of the project in guiding me into Heidegger. J. Donald Moon read several chapters and provided me with extensive and invaluable comments. A subtle influence was also exerted by Fred Dallmayr, for whom I had the pleasure of editing a *Festschrift* during the same time that I was working on this book. Invaluable insights and suggestions for revision came from those who read the entire manuscript: my colleague Tim Luke, Bill Connolly, and Raymond Geuss. Sincere thanks go to all of these people.

My editor at Cambridge University Press, Emily Loose, could not have been more helpful and competent. Maxine Riley, Terry Kingrea, Kim Hedge, and Kathy Akers, the secretaries in the Department of Political Science, showed, as always, consummate skill and unfailing patience in getting innumerable drafts through word processing. Help of various sorts also came from my graduate assistants, Scott Madsen and Helen Thompson. Finally, I am grateful for the deep support of my family: Pat, Lydia, and Cam.

Parts of Chapter 2 appeared in "Poststructuralism and Political Reflection," *Political Theory* 16 (May 1988), pp. 186–208, reprinted with permission. Parts of Chapters 3 and 4 appeared in "Heidegger and the Difficulties of a Postmodern Ethics and Politics," *Political Theory* 18 (February 1990), pp. 80–103, reprinted with permission. And a very early version of portions of Chapter 7 appeared in "Justice and the Postmodern Problematic," *Praxis International* 7 (October 1987–January 1988), pp. 306–19, reprinted with permission. I also gratefully acknowledge permission to reprint a portion of Martin Heidegger, "Language," *Poetry, Language, Thought,* ed. by Alfred Hofstadter (New York: Harper and Row, 1971), pp. 198–9.

-≫ ⊱-

INTRODUCTION: THE
POSTMODERN PROBLEMATIC

What does it mean to be "postmodern" or reflect upon things in a "postmodern" way? The possible answers are numerous. The term "postmodern," as well as its companions "postmodernity" and "postmodernism," are used in relation to a wide variety of phenomena in and claims about art, architecture, literature, philosophy, society, and politics. What one decides to emphasize as important within this constellation will, of course, depend on one's interests and intentions. Since there already exist numerous discussions that attempt to survey the field of things circulating under the various "post-" rubrics, I want to proceed directly to the drawing of some distinctions that will help provide initial bearings for those primarily concerned with ethics and politics.[1]

From this point of view, it is useful to distinguish first between oppositional and nonoppositional modes of postmodern thought and action.[2] This distinction is only a rough one, if for no other

[1] Useful surveys are contained in the special issues on postmodernism of *Cultural Critique* 5 (Winter 1986–7) and *Theory, Culture and Society* No. 23 (June 1988); in Andrew Ross, ed. *Universal Abandon: The Politics of Postmodernism* (Minneapolis: University of Minnesota Press, 1988); in Wolfgang Welsch, *Unsere postmoderne Moderne* (Weinheim: VCH, 1987); and in David Harvey, *The Condition of Postmodernity* (Oxford: Basil Blackwell, 1989), ch. 3.
[2] See Hal Foster, "Postmodernism: A Preface," *The Anti-Aesthetic: Essays on Postmodern Culture* (Port Townsend, Wash.: Bay Press, 1983), p. xii.

reason than that to be *post*modern in any sense means to stand away from, or in opposition to, *something* modern. Nevertheless, the questioning and opposition of some thinkers runs deeper than that of others and has a more radical ethical–political edge. Perhaps the least oppositional mode of postmodern thought is manifested in much of what is taken in the United States to be postmodern architecture. The primary thing it opposes is a particular school of modernist architecture, the International Style. At its worst, this new stance boils down to a much greater acceptance of ornamentation on buildings and a penchant for mixing traditional styles with contemporary ones. But even within architecture, there are more oppositional ways of construing what it means to be postmodern; ways that question more thoroughly the dominant rules by which the modern architect has operated, and the standard ways architecture has been related to the dominant imperatives of political and economic systems.[3]

When one moves from architecture to philosophy and social theory, the asymmetry is reversed; the oppositional wing is far stronger. One reason for this is that the widely diffused post-structuralist methods developed by philosophers like Foucault and Derrida seem to dispose those who use them to a kind of perpetual criticism that cuts deeply and broadly into the foundations of modernity. It is this more oppositional sort of postmodern philosophical reflection that interests me.

What are the foundations or deep structures of modernity that postmodern philosophers attack? An answer to this question can quickly balloon to the same proportions as one about the meaning of "postmodern." However, if one keeps the focus on what is most directly relevant to ethics and politics, an answer of manageable proportions can be sketched fairly easily. A first target of attack is the distinctive emphasis in modernity on a particular way in which human beings should relate to the world. In early modern thinkers such as Descartes and Hobbes, one sees this relation beginning to emerge clearly. The individual subject is conceived of as an isolated mind and will; and his vocation is to get clear about the world, to bring it under the

3 An interesting attempt to illustrate what is involved in a more radical notion of postmodern architecture is Bernard Tschumi, *Cinegramme Folie: Le Parc de la Villette* (Princeton, N.J.: Princeton Architectural Press, 1987). A useful overview of the more mainstream type of postmodern architecture is contained in Harvey, *The Condition of Postmodernity*, ch. 4.

control of reason and thus make it available for human projects. The modern world, says Derrida, stands under the imperative of giving a rational account of everything; or, as Foucault more ominously puts it, of interrogating everything.[4] This modern orientation toward a reason aimed at enhancing human will and control has no limits. It manifests itself finally in the twentieth century as a "will to planetary order."[5]

Such a constellation of reason and will was a necessary precondition for the successful emergence of industrial capitalism in the nineteenth century. As critics in that century already saw quite clearly, capitalism was not just a new way of producing things, but also a logic of rationalization that corroded all traditions and called all aspects of social and cultural life to account. Moreover, the logic of capitalism became intertwined with the Enlightenment faith in material and moral progress. The legitimacy of the modern world thereafter anchored itself in the promise of "will as infinite enrichment," on the one hand, and the promise of justice for the individual in the liberal state, on the other.[6]

These hallmarks of Western modernity, capitalism and the liberal state, came under radical attack from socialism and Marxism. However, from the point of view of postmodern thinkers, these criticisms did not cut deeply enough into the basic modern orientation of reason and will. Thus Marxism becomes just as much a target of postmodern attack as capitalism and the liberal state. In Marxism the will to mastery is merely transferred to a collective level: to the will of the proletariat to master history. And the rationality behind this will ends up manifesting itself in the twentieth century in the form of those immense bureaucratic states for which the Soviet Union was the first model. The threat of the possessive individual will and the corrosive logic of capitalism was to be tamed; but the tamer became a new threat. The promise of worker emancipation from capitalism thus ended up merely giving the screw of will and reason a further turn.

4 See especially Derrida, "The Principle of Reason: The University in the Eyes of Its Pupils," *Diacritics* XIX (Fall 1983), pp. 7ff.
5 Heidegger, *Hölderlins Hymnen "Germanien" und "Der Rhein,"* Vol. 39, *Gesamtausgabe* (Frankfurt: Klostermann, 1980), p. 23 and *Hölderlins Hymne "Der Ister,"* Vol. 53, *Gesamtausgabe* (Frankfurt: Klostermann, 1984), p. 59.
6 Jean-François Lyotard, "Rules and Paradoxes and Svelte Appendix," *Cultural Critique* 5 (Winter 1986–7), p. 215.

The questioning of modern foundations is not something oc-curring only in the pages of academic texts. The claim of post-moderns is that it is happening as well out there in society. Ex-actly what is happening and to what degree, however, is a matter of dispute. Use of the term "postmodernity" seems to imply that so much of modernity's cognitive and social structures have changed that we can speak of a new historical period. But that claim is probably too strong. Perhaps most would see the sorts of changes we are experiencing as putting us in a situation of "post-modern modernity."[7] This implies that our modernity is riven by phenomena that are not easily comprehended within familiar cognitive and social structures. If the term is awkward and am-biguous, so is the social reality it claims to describe.[8]

As a way of keeping an emphasis on such ambiguity and uncer-tainty, I want to refer to the phenomena at issue here with the term "postmodern problematic." Four interrelated phenomena constitute the bulk of this problematic: the increasing incredulity toward metanarratives, the growing awareness of new problems wrought by societal rationalization, the explosion of new informa-tional technologies, and the emergence of new social movements. Together these phenomena constitute an uncertain mixture of challenges, dilemmas, and opportunities that form a distinctive context for contemporary ethical–political reflection.[9]

I. Increasing incredulity toward metanarratives

Perhaps the most well-known short description of postmodern-ism is that provided by Jean-François Lyotard: "incredulity to-

7 I use here part of the title of Wolfgang Welsch's very useful book, *Unsere postmoderne Moderne.*

8 Derrida maintains that the security of all that is near and dear "is trembling today" in "The Ends of Man," in *Margins of Philosophy,* ed. and trans. by Alan Bass (Chicago: University of Chicago Press, 1982), p. 133. For a work that orients itself around a Foucault-inspired analysis of ambiguity, see William Connolly, *The Politics of Ambiguity* (Madison: University of Wisconsin Press, 1987).

9 My stress on the ambiguity and uncertainty characteristic of "our postmodern modernity" should not be understood as denying that a certain degree of trembling and casting about for self-reassurance has accompanied modern consciousness, at least since the French Revolution. See Habermas's argument in *The Philosophical Discourse of Modernity: Twelve Lectures,* trans. by Frederick Lawrence (Cambridge, Mass.: MIT Press, 1987). However, even Habermas is struck by the "new obscurity" of our situation. See his "The New Obscurity," *Philosophy and Social Criticism* 11 (Winter 1986), pp. 1–18.

ward metanarratives."[10] By "metanarratives" or "master narratives," Lyotard means those foundational interpretive schemes that have constituted the ultimate and unquestioned sources for the justification of scientific–technological and political projects in the modern world. Such narratives, focusing on God, nature, progress, and emancipation, are the anchors of modern life.

Lyotard has emphasized that he is describing not so much a new historical period as "a mood, or better a state of mind."[11] It may be useful to draw a further distinction at this point, one that I think is not entirely foreign to Lyotard's intentions. In a narrow sense, one can speak of a resistant state of mind shared by intellectuals and ordinary people alike who feel dominated by, and work to combat, the way modern metanarratives represent reality. For philosophers and social theorists, this state of mind manifests itself in such methods of critique as genealogy and deconstruction. Although this resistance is sharpest in the work of contemporary French philosophers, it is a mistake to see it as limited to them. Without blending out the distinctiveness of their contribution, it is important to keep in mind how broad the current of incredulity has become in the post–World War II era.

In the late 1940s, the ideal of the good life spawned by infinite scientific–technological progress was subjected to penetrating critiques by Martin Heidegger, as well as Max Horkheimer and Theodor Adorno.[12] In the 1960s and 1970s, deeply embedded metanarratives surrounding the relations of men and women came under unprecedented attack from feminists.[13] The liberal tradition as a whole also found itself in philosophi-

---

10 Lyotard, *The Postmodern Condition: A Report on Knowledge,* trans. by G. Bennington and B. Massumi (Minneapolis: University of Minnesota Press, 1984), p. xxiv.

11 Lyotard, "Rules and Paradoxes and Svelte Appendix." pp. 209–10.

12 Martin Heidegger, *The Question Concerning Technology and Other Essays,* trans. by William Lovitt (New York: Harper and Row, 1969); and Max Horkheimer and Theodor Adorno, *The Dialectic of Enlightenment,* trans. by John Cummings (New York: Herder and Herder, 1972).

13 For a sampling of the feminist challenge, see Alison Jagger and Paula T. Rothenberg, eds., *Feminist Frameworks: Alternative Theoretical Accounts of the Relations Between Women and Men,* 2nd ed. (New York: McGraw-Hill, 1984). For a recent consideration of feminism and traditional metanarratives in relation to postmodernism, see Nancy Fraser and Linda J. Nicholson, "Social Criticism without Philosophy: An Encounter between Feminism and Postmodernism," in Linda J. Nicholson, ed., *Feminism/Postmodernism* (New York: Routledge, 1990).

cal question during the 1970s and 1980s. Although critiques of
liberalism were hardly new, those that arose in the wake of John
Rawls's *A Theory of Justice* generated a new level of uncertainty
for that tradition and its perspective on justice. Here I am
referring in particular to the attacks leveled at the notion of
universally valid "primary goods" that formed the cornerstone
of Rawls's original account of justice. The critiques of this notion have forced liberals to see that the diversity of basic goods
is a much deeper problem than they had thought, and thus that
the problem of just institutions is also more complex.[14] Marxism, the traditional Western answer to the failures of liberalism,
has itself been brought under greater suspicion than ever before, as I suggested earlier. This suspicion goes deeper than the
classical critiques, because it locates difficulties in Marxism even
when it is interpreted in a sympathetic way.[15] The result of
these recent critiques is to make Marxism look far too much in
complicity with our modern productivist culture and its conceptual anchors.[16]

One thing that emerges from all these instances of mounting
incredulity is a heightened awareness of how strongly Western
thought is oriented to the consciousness of a subject (singular or
collective) who is faced with the task of surveying, subduing, and
negotiating *his* way through a world of objects, other subjects,
and his own body. Here, of course, is where recent French
thought has applied itself most persistently, trying to show both
how our traditional modes of thinking privilege the rational,
willful subject and what costs this entails.

The resistant state of mind often manifests itself among postmoderns in a way that is maximally "impertinent" to the shibbo-
leths of modernity. The rationale for this tone is to shock or jolt
the addressee into seeing the contestable quality of what he takes

14 John Rawls, *A Theory of Justice* (Cambridge, Mass.: Harvard University Press,
1971). For the critiques, see especially Michael Sandel, *Liberalism and the Limits
of Justice* (Cambridge: Cambridge University Press, 1982); and Michael
Walzer, *Spheres of Justice: A Defense of Pluralism and Justice* (New York: Basic
Books, 1983).

15 A typical classical critique is Karl Popper, *The Open Society and Its Enemies*. Vol.
2 (Oxford: Oxford University Press, 1949).

16 For a sample of recent critiques, see Habermas, "Remarks on Hegel's Jena
Philosophy," in *Theory and Practice*, trans. by John Viertel (Boston: Beacon
Press, 1973); and Jean Baudrillard, *For a Critique of the Political Economy of the
Sign*, trans. by Charles Levin (St. Louis: Telos Press, 1981), and *The Mirror of
Production*, trans. by Mark Poster (St. Louis: Telos Press, 1975).

as a certainty.[17] But there is a danger when the resistant state of mind lets this tone predominate. What I mean by this is that there is sometimes a loss of attention to a broader, more diffuse "state of mind" that inheres in our postmodern modernity. Here Lyotard's first choice of terms, "mood," is perhaps more apt. It is this mood and the attempts to turn it in an affirmative direction that constitute the most subtle challenge to modern ethical–political reflection. The mood is partially anxious and melancholy: Postmodern reflection knows we really are "homeless." But such reflection also often manifests the feeling that somehow there is something affirmative emerging, something to be celebrated. Nietzsche is frequently looked to for insights at this point. Without implying that that is the wrong source, I am going to look rather to Heidegger. I will try to draw out of his work an initial sense of this peculiarly ambiguous mood of melancholy/delight and show how it might help in understanding what learning to be at home in homelessness might mean.

II. New awareness of dangers of societal rationalization

The erosion of the credibility of foundational metanarratives has increasingly helped bring into sharper focus a social and political problem of vast proportions. The costs of Western modernization or rationalization are being progressively reestimated upward. Prominent among such reevaluations are Foucault's analysis of the process of "normalization," Habermas's of "the colonization of the lifeworld," and Lyotard's of the logic of "performativity."[18] These reevaluations draw attention to (among other things) prob-

17 I borrow the term "impertinence," as well as the explanation of its systematic role in postmodern thinking, from Michael Shapiro, "Weighing Anchor: Postmodern Journeys from the Life-World," in Stephen K. White, ed., *Life-World and Politics: Between Modernity and Postmodernity* (Notre Dame, Ind.: University of Notre Dame Press, 1989), pp. 146ff. Shapiro emphasizes only the "benefits" of impertinence; I wish, however, to indicate as well a potential "cost" that sometimes threatens to disable some of the best insights postmodernism offers.

18 Michel Foucault, *Discipline and Punish* (New York: Random House, 1977), pp. 170, 182–4, 208–9, 222, 224; *The History of Sexuality*, Vol. 1, *An Introduction* (New York: Random House, 1980), Part Five; Habermas, *The Theory of Communicative Action*, Vol. 2, *Lifeworld and System: A Critique of Functionalist Reason* (Boston: Beacon Press, 1988), Ch. 8; and Lyotard, *Postmodern Condition*, pp. 47–67.

lems associated with the growth of the welfare activities of the modern state. They recognize that, however benevolent these activities may be in intention, the discourses and institutions that emerge with them often promote a deep and progressive disempowerment of their clients. For theorists from the center to the left, this insight signals a need for thorough self-reexamination. It must be emphasized, however, that such an insight is not equivalent to the standard conservative warnings about the evils of modern state power. It is different because it is coupled with a recognition that the discourses and institutions of corporate capitalism also participate in a logic of disempowerment. And it is only this *dual* concern that characterizes the recognition of a postmodern problematic.

This questioning of the welfare state is also different from traditional Marxist critiques, since the latter gained their plausibility and normative bite from assumptions about the superiority of an alternative form of society. For those who take the postmodern problematic seriously, the comfort of such assumptions is not available, since there is little reason to believe that such whole cloth alternatives will not blindly reproduce disempowering modes of rationalization under new guises.[19] A serious confrontation with the postmodern challenge thus requires one to be, paradoxically, both more radical and less radical when considering political alternatives.

III. New informational technologies

A third element of the postmodern problematic is the rise of new informational technologies, by which I mean all forms of media, beginning especially with television, that vastly enhance the circulation of images and information. From my perspective, what makes these technologies problematic is their political ambivalence.[20] On the one hand, they are often seen as instruments for

19 Here one can see the difference between current critiques of societal rationalization and earlier ones emerging out of the Marxist tradition, such as Herbert Marcuse, *One-Dimensional Man* (Boston: Beacon Press, 1964). However far Marcuse was from orthodox Marxism, it was his faith in the possibility of a totally different society that breathed life into his critiques.

20 Lyotard, *Postmodern Condition*, pp. 66–7; Habermas, *Theory of Communicative Action*, Vol. 2, pp. 571–3; and Timothy Luke, "Informationalism and Ecology," *Telos* 56 (Summer 1983), pp. 59–73.
   The dimensions of informationalization and societal rationalization are

empowering individuals, a view clearly evident in the IBM television commercial in the 1980s that showed a Charlie Chaplin look-alike bringing his life into order with the help of a personal computer. The message, of course, was that because of new informational technology, postmodern times will be better than modern times. A parallel view holds that the decentralizing potential of some of the newest technology can also enhance the prospects for radically democratizing political life.[21] On the other hand, informational technology is just as often seen as the instrument of an emerging Big Brother or a potent new ideological apparatus of corporate capitalism. What these opposing views have in common is an agreement on the power of such technologies to structure the consciousness and self-identity of individuals and groups. What they disagree about is the question of who will likely control these technologies and what purposes they will serve.

But to state the issue so baldly is to miss the full extent of the ambiguities involved. Certainly one can envision greater possibilities for democratized forms of control in micro- as opposed to macrocomputers, in decentralizing advances in videotechnology, desktop publishing, and so forth; but even assuming some progressive potential here, it is likely that most informational technology will remain linked to large institutions, both public and private, and thus to the expansion of societal rationalization. Therefore it might appear that such technology will in fact function more as a potent means for enhancing the ideological control of dominant groups or classes. But again, such a straightforward reading of informationalization underplays the ambiguities and obscurities involved. Perhaps the problem is better seen not so much in terms of a single hegemonic code of "bourgeois ideology" into which we are socialized, but rather in terms of a proliferation of codes.[22] The crucial questions then become how

especially emphasized by Mark Poster in his useful attempt to understand contemporary social reality in a way that employs the insights of poststructuralism to supplement the sort of critique traditionally associated with the Frankfurt School; see *Critical Theory and Poststructuralism: In Search of a Context* (Ithaca, N.Y.: Cornell University Press, 1989).

21 See Benjamin Barber, *Strong Democracy: Participatory Politics for a New Age* (Berkeley: University of California Press, 1984), ch. 10.

22 On the fragmentation and diffusion of consciousness, see David Held, "Crisis Tendencies, Legitimation and the State," in John Thompson and David Held, eds., *Habermas: Critical Debates* (Cambridge, Mass.: MIT Press, 1982), pp. 189ff; and *The Theory of Communicative Action*, Vol. 2, pp. 354–5.

this proliferation is structured, which cognitive and behavioral scripts are privileged, and which segments of society are systematically advantaged or disadvantaged in the process.

If considerations such as these have any validity, then the informational revolution adds new and perplexing dimensions to the rethinking of questions of power, ideology, freedom, and justice, a rethinking that has already become more obscure in light of the problems emerging from the upward reestimation of the costs of societal rationalization.

IV. New social movements

The fourth phenomenon is the appearance of new values and "new social movements" in Western industrialized societies.[23] Social scientists have for some time been calling attention to the emergence of "postmaterialist values" and new sorts of groups, for whom politics is not in the first instance a matter of compensations that the corporate economy

> or welfare state can provide, but of defending and restoring endangered ways of life. In short, the new conflicts are not ignited by *distribution problems*, but by questions having to do with the *grammar of forms of life*.[24]

The women's movement, antinuclear movement, radical ecologists, ethnic movements, homosexuals, and countercultural groups in general all share, at least to some degree, this new status, even if they differ in many substantive ways. They all have a somewhat defensive character, as well as a focus on struggling to gain the ability to construct socially their own collective identity, characteristics that make them rather anomalous in relation to the standard rules for interest group behavior in the modern state. On the other hand, though, they are just as anomalous for Marxian-influenced theories of the left that continually seek the social embodiment of a revolutionary subjectivity that

23 On "new social movements," see the special issue of *Social Research* on this topic, especially the article by Jean Cohen, "Strategy of Identity: New Theoretical Paradigms and Contemporary Social Movements," *Social Research* 52 (Winter 1985), pp. 663–716. On "postmaterialist" values, see Ronald Inglehart, *The Silent Revolution: Changing Values and Political Styles among Western Publics* (Princeton, N.J.: Princeton University Press, 1977).

24 Habermas, *The Theory of Communicative Action*, Vol. 2., p. 392; my emphasis.

will speak and act in the name of *all* disaffected groups. What stands out about new social movements is an irreducible pluralism and a suspicion of totalistic revolutionary programs.

For such groups, the growth of incredulity toward traditional metanarratives is particularly unlikely to be seen as a source of fear and trembling, but instead as a source of some cognitive space within which new orientations may have a better chance to flourish.[25] This is especially clear in the case of the women's movement and radical ecologists. Likewise, such groups are likely to be the most sensitive in regard to societal rationalization processes that threaten these spaces with closure.[26] Thus it is not surprising that the characteristics of such new social movements have been paid increasing attention by philosophers and social theorists who hope for a future where both the "normalizing" processes of the corporate capitalist, welfare state system, and the repressive closures of revolutionary systems are actively resisted.[27] The qualities of new social movements make them the most plausible immediate addressees of those theorists who celebrate the emergence of "local" resistance (Foucault), a "border conflict" (Habermas), "local determinism" (Lyotard), and particularistic "lines of flight" (DeLeuze) from the societal or revolutionary rationalization of life.[28]

Moreover, it is likely that these groups will have an especially strong interest in new informational technology, both because its decentralizing potential can foster more autonomous means of collective identity formation and because its rationalization-enhancing potential can simultaneously hinder such efforts.

25 The lack of skeptical orientation toward traditional metanarratives is one reason I do not include religious fundamentalists within the category of new social movements, however important they may be sociologically and politically. Moreover, such groups have, at best, an extremely selective sensitivity in regard to the dangers of societal rationalization.

26 See Jean Elshtain's critique of "liberal feminism" in *Public Man, Private Woman* (Princeton, N.J.: Princeton University Press, 1980); and Kathy Ferguson's feminist critique of bureaucratization in *The Feminist Case Against Bureaucracy* (Philadelphia: Temple University Press, 1984).

27 See Timothy Luke, "Class Contradictions and Social Cleavages in Informationalizing Post-Industrial Societies: On the Rise of New Social Movements," *New Political Science* 16–17 (Fall–Winter 1989), pp. 126–53.

28 Foucault, *History of Sexuality*, pp. 95–6; Habermas, *The Philosophical Discourse of Modernity: Twelve Lectures* (Cambridge, Mass.: MIT Press; 1987), pp. 360–6 (my translation); Lyotard, *Postmodern Condition*, p. xxiv; and Theodore Mills Norton, "Line of Flight: Gilles Deleuze, or Political Science Fiction," *New Political Science* 15 (Summer 1985), pp. 77–93.

V. Initial directions

To anyone who has followed the controversies surrounding post-modernism, my enumeration of the dimensions of a postmodern problematic will hardly be seen as startlingly original. Of course, the point is not to be original here, but rather to fix a plausible range of key issues. In fixing such a range, one then has a standard against which contributions to rethinking ethics and politics can be weighed. The more dimensions of the problematic addressed, the better the contribution.

A note of caution should be emphasized at this point. The fixing of a range of postmodern issues should not be taken as implying that traditional modern issues relating to ethics and politics thereby somehow lose their importance. Struggles between labor and capital and familiar controversies over civil liberties, for example, should not drop below the threshold of theoretical attention. The reconceptualizations I am seeking should not only address the new problematic, but also should be able to draw connections with old problematics.

If one seeks to address the postmodern problematic, where does one get the perspective to do so? It could be argued that a given strain of thought, say Foucault's, is adequate in this regard. I doubt, however, if any single existing position can bear this weight. One could, alternatively, examine various perspectives, distinguishing helpful from unhelpful insights. However, such a procedure is likely to make good sense only after at least some initial theoretical orientation is provided. My efforts in this book will be directed predominantly to fleshing out some concepts that will anchor just this sort of orientation.

But where does one look for such conceptual anchors when one aspect of the postmodern problematic – the incredulity toward metanarratives – has rendered traditional candidates suspect? The following chapter suggests a possible way of engaging this problem.

UNDERSTANDING THE
MODERN–POSTMODERN TENSION

The most prevalent set of intellectual strategies for undermining the status of traditional metanarratives can be gathered under the term "post-structuralism." The claims of post-structuralists, such as Foucault and Derrida, have been contested on many grounds. Here I only want to consider the controversy between these theorists and more traditional ways of thinking about ethical–political reflection. My claim is that, in probing this controversy, one can draw out certain distinctions that allow one to see more clearly what is at stake in the postmodernism debates, as well as realize why each side of the debate needs the other if we are to move toward more adequate modes of practical reflection.

I. The battle lines

How should post-structuralism inform ethical–political reflection? This is a complex and difficult question. The reason has to do with the radical quality of the insights generated by post-structuralism. Because of this quality, one cannot begin to answer the question satisfactorily in either of two straightforward ways.

On the one hand, an attempt could be made to render the insights of post-structuralism directly into the various idioms of ethical–political reflection as it has been traditionally conceived. The problem with this strategy is that it becomes merely a new manifestation of exactly what post-structuralism has seen to be the implicit authoritarianism of Western, "logocentric" thinking; in short, we would be demanding that post-structuralists give an account of themselves so that we could "discipline" them in such a way as to make them more pliant contributors to our basic, traditional tasks of analyzing the nature of action, rationality, subjectivity, ethical principles, institutions, processes, and so on. We thereby would become engaged in an imperialistic project of forcing post-structuralism to speak our traditional language, to accommodate itself to our standard, foundational distinctions: rational/irrational, legitimate/illegitimate, and so forth. The cognitive machinery of traditional ethical–political reflection would thus be allowed to operate upon post-structuralism in such a way that the latter would likely appear to be rather incoherent.[1]

Alternatively, one could look at this cognitive machinery from the viewpoint of the post-structuralists. But this route has its drawbacks as well, as I show after giving a brief characterization of post-structuralism, at least as it appears in the work of Michel Foucault and Jacques Derrida. Once the liabilities of a thoroughgoing post-structuralist approach have been elucidated, I attempt to explore in more detail why there is such a deep and recurrent tension between post-structuralism and traditional modes of ethical–political thinking.

Any brief characterization of post-structuralism is highly contestable. Mine simply has the goal of highlighting some themes that appear to be of particular interest to ethics and politics. With that caveat in mind, one can start the story with the structural linguistics of Ferdinand de Saussure in the early part of this century. Rather than trying to understand meaning according to the traditional model by analyzing the relationship of words to their referents (i.e., things in the world), Saussure began to tie meaning more to the relationship of signs (words being merely one type of sign) to one another. It is from the differences between signs in a system of signs that the meaning of any given

---

1 See the exchange between Charles Taylor and William Connolly: Taylor, "Foucault on Freedom and Truth," *Political Theory* (May 1984), pp. 152–83; Connolly, "Taylor, Foucault and Otherness," pp. 365–76; and Taylor, "Connolly, Foucault and Truth," *Political Theory* 13 (August 1985), pp. 377–85.

sign arises.[2] "The structuralist method, then, assumes that meaning is made possible by the existence of underlying systems of
conventions which enable elements to function individually as
signs." Structuralist analysis thus often took the form of developing models of such systems. In the social sciences, perhaps the
most well-known are Levi-Strauss's models of myths and kinship
systems.[3]

Such models, whether of social or literary texts, promised to
provide the net within which the meaning of particular actions,
practices, or passages could be captured. Structuralist analysis
typically made such meaning emerge within the logical workings
of key sets of binary oppositions: raw/cooked, nature/culture,
man/woman, light/dark, and so on.[4] Against this background,
the point of post-structuralism can be understood as the displacement of the status of such foundational, meaning-endowing
oppositions. Derrida's idea of deconstruction thus refers to deconstructing such oppositions: showing how their claimed foundational character collapses or undermines itself when they are
thought through.[5]

Derrida's insight here constitutes not just an attack on structuralism; rather, he found that this habit of starting with unquestioned binary oppositions is a characteristic of the dominant currents of Western, "metaphysical" thinking in general.
And Western *political* thought is certainly deeply implicated
here. This has been nicely illustrated, for example, by Michael
Ryan's deconstruction of Hobbes's foundational opposition between reason and the clear use of language, on the one hand,
and unreason and the ambiguous and metaphorical use of language, on the other. The first half of the opposition delimits
the sphere of what is privileged and foundational for the con-

2 Ferdinand de Saussure, *Course in General Linguistics,* trans. by Wade Baskin
  (London: Peter Owen, 1974).
3 Robert Young, "Post-Structuralism: An Introduction," in Young, ed., *Untying
  the Text* (London: Routledge and Kegan Paul, 1981), p. 3.
4 Terry Eagleton, *Literary Theory: An Introduction* (Minneapolis: University of
  Minnesota Press, 1983), pp. 133ff.
5 See, for example, Derrida's statements in *Positions* (Chicago: University of Chicago Press, 1981), pp. 6, 41. The way I have characterized the relationship
  between structuralism and post-structuralism implies a fairly sharp break. The
  fact that there is probably as much if not more continuity between them is
  thoughtfully elaborated by Jonathan Culler, *On Deconstruction: Theory and Criticism after Structuralism* (Ithaca, N.Y.: Cornell University Press, 1982), pp. 17–
  30, 222–5.

struction of a secure political world; the second half, the sphere of what is marginal, suspicious, and ultimately seditious – what post-structuralists often refer to as the "Other."

Ryan deconstructs Hobbes's imposing edifice by pointing out that it undermines its own authority by appealing at the start to the metaphor of a leviathan. "Hobbes' entire theory, then, rests on a linguistic form – metaphorical displacement, transposition and analogy – that he will later exclude and banish as seditious."[6] Ryan illustrates well how the use of deconstruction has an intrinsically political character. The method always takes what is claimed to be authoritative, logical, and universal and breaks those claims down, exposing arbitrariness, ambiguity, and conventionality – in short, exposing a power phenomenon where it was claimed that only reason existed.

Thus, one can say that the practice of deconstruction always has a politicizing effect. For present purposes, this insight means that the cognitive machinery of political thought is exposed as less reason-driven and more power-driven than was previously realized. Having said this, however, can one go on to say anything more about the implications of deconstruction for political reflection? Here it is interesting to consider how Derrida has responded to attempts by others to draw out further implications. When faced with a choice between two sets of cognitive machinery for orienting political thought and judgment, he responds by moving to "a deeper level of analysis which interrogates the conditions of possibility shared by both"; that is, which exposes a more basic cognitive machinery that, in turn, generates just this delimited choice situation.[7] This sort of intellectual move is archetypical for the deconstructionist. In effect, it constitutes a sort of "perpetual withholding operation."[8] This strategy is one of the main sources of deconstruction's provocative insights, but it is also the source of much frustration on the part of someone inquiring about political implications, for it can be interpreted as a strategy for avoiding certain sorts of questions that anyone concerned with politics and political reflection must face. Here is where the suspicion begins

6 Michael Ryan, *Marxism and Deconstruction: A Critical Articulation* (Baltimore, Md.: Johns Hopkins University Press, 1982), p. 4.
7 Nancy Fraser, "The French Derrideans: Politicizing Deconstruction or Deconstructing Politics," *New German Critique* 33 (Fall 1984), pp. 134–7.
8 Allan Megill, *Prophets of Extremity: Nietzsche, Heidegger, Foucault, Derrida* (Berkeley: University of California Press, 1985), p. 271.

to emerge that post-structuralists cannot give coherent answers to such questions.

One is back now at that initial dilemma: One either follows post-structuralism down a trail that persistently shies away from important political questions, or one finds some way of domesticating it and forcing it onto more familiar conceptual ground. Before I suggest a way to rethink this dilemma, it must be shown that the same difficulty arises out of Foucault's work. At first glance, this might not seem to be the case. His work is more politically and historically focused than Derrida's. Although he continually deconstructs hierarchical distinctions such as reason/madness and normal/abnormal, his underlying intention (at least in his later work) is to show how social institutions give practical force to such discursive distinctions and how such distinctions are reconstituted in radically different ways in different historical periods.[9] Thus, for example, in examining the discourse of criminality, he analyzes the significance of the emergence of the prison in the nineteenth century for the establishment of our distinction between normal and abnormal, as well as how changing conceptions of criminality gave rise to a new object of state power. The criminal, as he begins to emerge in the late eighteenth century, is no longer simply the isolated threat to royal power, on whose body the king must inscribe his vengeance through torture, but rather becomes the deviant from dominant social norms who in turn must become the object of extended surveillance, discipline, and therapeutic correction.

It has usually been assumed that with this shift in discourse there came a growing humanization of penal practice. But Foucault, as always, wants to turn our humanist self-congratulations into self-doubt, to show us that any new discourse is always also another new mode of power. For Foucault, this insight about "power/knowledge" is not just a general philosophical thesis, it is also a thesis about modernity. He sees the modern world as one in which power is insinuating itself into our lives in ways that we are not able to grasp very well with the traditional cognitive machinery of political thought.

In one sense, Foucault would agree that contemporary West-

9 See especially Michel Foucault, *Discipline and Punish: The Birth of the Prison*, trans. by Alan Sheridan (New York: Random House, 1977), and *The History of Sexuality*, Vol. 1, *An Introduction*, trans. by Robert Hurley (New York: Random House, 1978).

ern society has seen a diminution of "state power," when by that
term we mean the arbitrary and repressive employment of
mechanisms of coercion. His key point, however, is that we must
understand power also in another way, namely, as a slowly
spreading net of normalization that invades our language, our
institutions, and even (and especially) our consciousness of ourselves as subjects. This sort of power does not so much repress,
in the purely negative sense, as it "constrains," if one uses this
term in its sense of persistently channeling activity. One is not so
much stopped from engaging in some activity as one is given
directions for how it is *normally* carried out, with these directions
typically being accorded some sort of scientific status. Power, in
short, becomes productive of action, not just prohibitive.[10]

Foucault's thinking about power in the modern world is extraordinarily provocative. As much work over the last few years has
shown, it is capable of being employed in a fairly straightforward
manner for analyzing various sorts of political phenomena.[11]
Nevertheless, as with Derrida, difficulties are encountered when
one attempts to engage in a fully Foucauldian mode of political
thinking. Again, one runs into a sort of perpetual withholding
gesture. Moreover, in Foucault's work, the effects of this operation are even more weighted with direct political implications.
The problem, as numerous critics have noted, is that his post-
structuralist analysis of power and subjectivity provides us with
no real way of drawing distinctions between political ideals and
movements that might be more legitimate, freedom-enhancing,
rational, and so on than others.[12] In effect, Foucault's position
seems to allow no normative criteria of better or worse; all we
can do is to trace the differences among discourses and their
power effects.[13]

As with Derrida, Foucault's position is a source of both frustration and insight. The insight results from Foucault's determined
attachment to the project of elucidating what William Connolly

10 Foucault, *Discipline and Punish*, pp. 79–81, 136–8, 208–9.
11 See, for example, Kathy Ferguson, *The Feminist Case against Bureaucracy* (Philadelphia: Temple University Press, 1984). For some general thoughts on the
value of this kind of analysis, see my "Poststructuralism and Political Reflection," *Political Theory* 16 (May 1988), pp. 197–200.
12 Taylor, "Foucault on Freedom and Truth," pp. 165, 172ff.
13 This does not mean that Foucault, any more than Derrida, was not personally
associated with various progressive movements.

has called "an ontology of discord."[14] If the underlying effect of our Western, cognitive machinery – political, philosophical, and psychological – has been to introduce clarity, metanarrational unity, and consensus into our lives, then Foucault's purpose can be described as that of elucidating how an Other is *always* pushed aside, marginalized, forcibly homogenized, and devalued as that cognitive machinery does its work. This Other may be other actors, external nature, or aspects of our own physical or psychological life; but in every case, Foucault awakens in us the experience of discord as otherness is generated.

II. Two senses of responsibility

These themes that emerge from the post-structuralism of Foucault and Derrida suffuse much of postmodern thinking. They orient its modes of analysis, determine its topics, and embed within it certain persistent difficulties. It is by probing these themes further that one can begin to see the outlines of a way of understanding the underlying impulses that manifest themselves in the debates about postmodernism.

At the beginning of this chapter I said that, in addressing the question about post-structuralism and political reflection, one sort of answer was likely to be unsatisfactory: that is, one that forces post-structuralism to translate its insights directly into an idiom compatible with the traditional cognitive machinery of political thought. Now it should be clear why another sort of answer is also likely to be unsatisfactory. A thoroughly post-structuralist approach to political thinking would be one dominated by what is in effect a perpetual withholding gesture. Is there another alternative that might draw on the insights of both post-structuralism and traditional political reflection without subordinating either, one that would allow both voices some expression? Later chapters give an affirmative answer to this question. However, the path to such an answer requires a deeper exploration of the nature of these two voices.

One way to open up this topic is to reflect further on the view that Foucault, especially in his genealogies, is engaged in the task of describing phenomena in a way that "incite[s] the experience of discord or discrepancy between the social construction of self,

14 Connolly, "Taylor, Foucault and Otherness," p. 371.

truth and rationality and that which does not fit neatly within their folds."[15] By proceeding in this way, Foucault is proving the reality of his ontological view indirectly, that is, by exposing the persistent and ineradicable, but submerged, presence of dissonance in our lives. Dissonance, in other words, is allowed to show itself to us, an experience that has an unsettling effect on our modern, deep-rooted quest for harmony and unity, for a world of problems finally solved.

I would suggest that this kind of ontological orientation is shared, at least implicitly, by most radical postmodern thinkers. If this is so, then one might understand their work as intellectual strategies that "bear witness" to this dissonance.[16] The strategies may be quite different, but they are drawn together by a strong sense of responsibility to expose and track the way our modern cognitive machinery operates to deny the ineradicability of dissonance. The harmony, unity, and clarity promised by this machinery have, for the postmodern, an inevitable cost; and that cost is couched in the language of an Other that is always engendered, devalued, disciplined, and so on, in the infinite search for a more tractable and ordered would. One might speak here of something like a moral–aesthetic sense of *responsibility to otherness*. Its moral dimension is most clearly evident when the Other attended to is a human being. But how one cultivates and responds to this sense in general goes beyond traditional moral reasoning in ways that seem to involve deeply aesthetic qualities.

It might seem at first glance that my strong emphasis on responsibility is a curious one, given the often repeated charge that poststructuralism or radical postmodernism is irresponsible. But things look less curious if one now distinguishes another sense of responsibility from which the postmodern does indeed want to distance herself – and thus risk the charge of a certain sort of irresponsibility. This sense is familiar in our modern, everyday life and implicit in the dominant, Western styles of ethical and political thought. It might be called a sense of *responsibility to act* in the world in a justifiable way, a moral-prudential obligation to acquire reliable knowledge and act to achieve practical ends in some defensible manner. This responsibility derives from the

---

15 Ibid., p. 368.
16 Jean François Lyotard, *The Differend: Phrases in Dispute*, trans. by George Van Den Abbeele (Minneapolis: University of Minnesota Press, 1988), pp. xiii, 140–1.

character of being in the world both physically and politically: from the need to survive physically, to avoid harm, to conform to time constraints, to realize certain values, and to meet the expectations of others. What the postmodern thinker wants to assert here is that meeting this responsibility always requires one, at some point, to fix or close down parameters of thought and to ignore or homogenize at least some dimensions of specificity or difference among actors. To act in this sense means inevitably closing off sources of possible insight and treating people as alike for the purpose of making consistent and defensible decisions about alternative courses of action. The modern thinker associates the commitment to this sense of responsibility with self-justification either in the sense of moral uprightness or pragmatic effectiveness. The postmodern thinker, however, sees a deeper, unacknowledged will to mastery at work here.

I try to make this distinction between the two senses of responsibility plausible in several stages throughout the book. The underlying intention in drawing it is to expose the most significant divergence between thinkers such as Foucault and proponents of more traditional modes of political reflection. The concern for otherness, as I define it here, has its roots in the classic critiques of modernity launched by Nietzsche, Heidegger, and Horkheimer and Adorno. My hope is to do justice to this strain of thinking without, however, accepting its strong implication that all modernist modes of thinking are equally infected with the disease of willful subjectivity. It should always be taken to be an open question how much a given perspective on ethics and politics – which responds to the responsibility to act – actually implies the dangers postmoderns have associated with subjectivity. A primary example of why this is necessary emerges in Habermas's work, in particular in his notion of a shift from a paradigm of subjectivity to one of intersubjectivity. Most postmoderns do not take this shift very seriously. Indeed, Habermas is one of their arch enemies, and an especially dangerous one because the disease of subjectivity is so cleverly disguised. This cavalier dismissal of Habermas's work is unwarranted. There are simply too many rich insights in his notion of communicative action and intersubjectivity to allow them to be washed wholesale into the great sink of subjectivity. I draw heavily – if implicitly – on these insights to construe the sense of responsibility to act, just as I draw heavily – and explicitly – on Heidegger to construe the responsibility to otherness. Habermas is helpful to the present project in two ways. First, he allows us to comprehend action and cooperation in ways that are not reducible to the model of the strategically behaving subject who monologically surveys his or her world in an objectivized manner. Second, his model of communicative action and intersubjectivity provides the most useful standard against which one can test postmodern claims about radically new orientations to ethics and politics.[17]

My deepest reservation about Habermas and other traditional orientations is fairly straightforward. They persist in the belief that the problem of otherness can be adequately settled within their frameworks.[18] However, no such framework can ever give us a closed set of procedures for accomplishing this task. And it is crucial to addressing the postmodern problematic satisfactorily that we let go of this belief. Here I side strongly with the postmoderns.

The perspective I have started to develop is intimately related to how one thinks about language. The focus on the responsibility to otherness and the responsibility to act is meant to mirror two different ways of understanding the connection between human beings and language. Language can be understood in terms of its *action-coordinating* or its *world-disclosing* capacity.

17 See Jürgen Habermas, *The Philosophical Discourse of Modernity: Twelve Lectures,* trans. by Frederick Lawrence (Cambridge, Mass.: MIT Press, 1987), and *The Theory of Communicative Action,* Vols. I and II, trans. and introduced by Thomas A. McCarthy (Boston: Beacon Press, 1984 and 1987).

For a sympathetic presentation of Habermas's model of communicative action, see my *The Recent Work of Jürgen Habermas: Reason, Justice and Modernity* (Cambridge: Cambridge University Press, 1988). A useful account of the overall controversy between Habermas and the French is contained in Mark Poster, *Critical Theory and Poststructuralism: In Search of a Context* (Ithaca, N.Y.: Cornell University Press, 1989), ch. 1.

18 This point came home most clearly to me when I presented a paper on this topic and a staunch Habermasian brushed my concerns aside with the claim that we could have virtual, "advocatory discourses" in which we represent those others who cannot in some sense effectively speak for themselves: the insane, children, past generations, future generations, those who have no sense of political efficacy, and so on. My answer is that one must certainly try to do this, but in doing it, we must carry a deeply tragic sense of the inevitable failures involved. Without this strong sense of affect emerging from the seriousness with which one takes the responsibility to otherness, one will always be susceptible to a subtle and blinding overconfidence. The declaration that the problem of otherness is solved by the use of the mechanism of virtual, advocatory discourses is perhaps something like a twentieth-century version of Britain's eighteenth-century assertion to the American colonists that they should be satisfied with virtual representation in Parliament.

These correspond, respectively, to the responsibility to act and the responsibility to otherness. A grasp of the importance of this language distinction, as well as of its relationship to the two senses of responsibility, can be achieved by examining the dispute between Derrida and Habermas.

III. Two dimensions of language

The action-coordinating approach to language is well represented by the work of Anglo-American philosophers like J. L. Austin and John Searle. The particular focus of their work has been on how language, in the form of speech acts, allows us to do things in the world. Austin and Searle have followed a strategy of analyzing how, in normal speech, our *saying* certain things allows us also to *do* certain things (e.g., saying "I promise" under the appropriate or normal conditions also constitutes the making of a promise). This capacity of speech acts to coordinate our interaction under normal, conventional conditions is what Austin called "illocutionary force."[19]

The Austin–Searle tradition has been attacked by Derrida. According to Derrida, this tradition and its insights focus on constructing distinctions between normal/abnormal, literal/figurative, or serious/fictive uses of language. In the former mode, language is performing its proper or main function. The latter mode is thereby taken to be derivative and secondary. Derrida's critique takes the expected form of a deconstruction of this distinction. In particular, he argues that the conventional conditions for normal speech usage can never be clearly delineated, for they are inexhaustibly open-textured. And if this is so, then normal speech is simply a variant or special case of abnormal speech. Or, to put it in a more provocative way, serious speech is merely a special case of fictive speech.[20]

The implications for social and political thought that emerge from this dispute between approaches to language that privilege either serious or fictive usage can be illuminated by look-

19 J. L. Austin, *How to Do Things with Words*, 2nd ed. (Cambridge, Mass.: Harvard University Press, 1975); John Searle, *Speech Acts* (Cambridge: Cambridge University Press, 1969).
20 Derrida, "Signature Event Context," in *Margins of Philosophy*, trans. by Alan Bass (Chicago: University of Chicago Press, 1982), pp. 321ff. For a lucid account of the ensuing controversy between Derrida and Searle, see Culler, *On Deconstruction*, pp. 110ff.

ing at the way Habermas has responded to Derrida's critique.[21] He has felt it necessary to respond, because he knows that the critique applies to his own work as well, in particular to his delineation of serious speech as that mode in which there are certain "idealized imputations" about the validity of what is said: its truth, its normative legitimacy, and its sincerity or authenticity. Only speech acts that accord (either explicitly or implicitly) with the "formal pragmatic" rules for raising and redeeming these validity claims constitute normal language use, which for Habermas means language use capable of sustaining "understanding-oriented action."[22]

For some time, Habermas has been trying to articulate a conception of action that grasps the special coordinating role of language, as well as the competence subjects display in ongoing, linguistically mediated behavior. For present purposes, what is important about Habermas's privileging of the notion of understanding-oriented or "communicative action" is that it aims at comprehending how the coordination of action is possible in ways not reducible to coordination based on complementary strategic positions of opposed subjects. From Habermas's point of view, what is seminal about Austin's work is that it discovered "a mechanism of action coordination in the illocutionary binding force [*Bindungskraft*] of linguistic utterance." For this binding force to take hold in everyday practice, speech must be subjugated to certain limitations. "These limitations, under which illocutionary acts develop an action-coordinating force and release action-relevant consequences, define the sphere of normal speech."[23]

As has been shown, in Austin's account these limitations took the form of conventional conditions for the success of speech acts. But as Derrida has pointed out, such conventional conditions are inexhaustibly open-textured, a fact that implies that the sphere of normal speech can never be clearly delineated. Habermas, however, argues that his own position is not open to this critique, since, on his account, the relevant conditions are not

---

21 Derrida is not the only postmodern thinker who explicitly makes such a critique. See Lyotard, "Rules and Paradoxes and Svelte Appendix," *Cultural Critique* 5 (Winter 1986–7), p. 218.

22 Jürgen Habermas, *The Philosophical Discourse of Modernity*, p. 196, my translation.

23 Ibid., pp. 195–6, my translation.

conventional, but rather those "idealized imputations" that characterize even "institutionally unbound speech actions."[24]

It is the underlying mutual expectation between actors that they can, if challenged, defend the specific claims they raise that, in turn, creates the "binding force" for the coordination of action. In fictive speech, however, this sytem of validity claims brought into play by illocutive acts is at least partially suspended. This "neutralization of the binding force unburdens the disempowered illocutionary acts from the decision pressure of communicative everyday practice; it suspends the sphere of ordinary speech and empowers [speech] for the playful creation of new worlds − or rather: for the pure demonstration of the world-disclosing power of innovative linguistic expressions."[25]

At this point, the connection noted earlier between two types of language use and the two types of responsibility can begin to be drawn out. The language distinction can be described as one between language that *coordinates action-in-the-world* and language that is *world-disclosing*. For Habermas, it is imperative that we give preeminence to the former. We get to the heart of what language is all about only if we approach it primarily "in terms of its problem-solving capacity for interaction."[26] With this assertion, one can see how, ultimately, Habermas's research program affirms the responsibility to act in the world.

Habermas argues that the deconstructionist's alternative privileging of the uncoordinating, world-disclosing capacity of language makes it unclear how one could ever account for the reproduction of social life in general and the occurrence of many learning processes that take place within it. The focus on world-*disclosing* gives one no adequate way of appreciating the fact that "linguistically mediated processes such as the attainment of knowledge, identity formation, socialization and social integration master problems *within the world*." Linguistic interaction "makes learning processes [in these dimensions] possible thanks to the idealizations" built into it. And it is within such learning processes that the world-disclosing power of language "must be *confirmed*." In the deconstructionist model, "the renew-

24 Ibid., pp. 196−9, my translation; and Habermas, *Communication and the Evolution of Society*, trans. by Thomas McCarthy (Boston: Beacon Press, 1979), pp. 38−9.
25 Habermas, *The Philosophical Discourse of Modernity*, p. 201, my translation.
26 Ibid., p. 205, my translation.

ing process of linguistic world-disclosure no longer has any *counter-pressure* from the confirming process of practice in the world."[27]

Thus Habermas focuses primarily on language's capacity to coordinate action to solve a range of "problems *within the world*," and the bounds of that world are the idealizations that ground normal speech. Habermas admits that these idealizations are fully in force only in the lifeworld of *modern* subjects, but their emergence in human history seems to be conceived as if it represents the coming of language to its essence. Language, as it were, has finally untangled itself sufficiently so that its essence – facilitating the coordination of action – can manifest itself with a smoothness impossible in premodern times.[28]

The post-structuralist response to this view is to question the status of Habermas's whole chain of concepts from normal speech to the idealizations. The deployment of those idealizations in modernity does not represent a crucial stage in the coming of language to its essence as a medium for action coordination, but rather merely one more episode in which we disclose to ourselves another way of seeing the world. Following Nietzsche, the post-structuralists would say that all the normality within a world is ultimately sustained by nothing more than fictions whose fictionality has been forgotten.[29] And this forgetting has the effect of denying the otherness that is spawned by *any* human construct.

One way to interpret the post-structuralist position here is simply as another form of antifoundationalism. It is indeed that, but it differentiates itself by a more thoroughgoing commitment to the world-disclosing quality of language. Other antifoundationalists, such as communitarian political theorists or philosophers like Rorty, would agree that Habermas's idealizations are fictions in the sense that they do not provide him with as solid a ground as he believes.[30] Thus, they recognize that there is no essence of

27 Ibid., pp. 204–7, my translation and emphasis.
28 See Habermas, "Reply to Critics," *Habermas: Critical Debates,* ed. by David Held and John B. Thompson (Cambridge, Mass.: MIT Press, 1982), p. 253; and "Questions and Counterquestions," *Praxis International* 4 (October 1984), pp. 229–49.
29 See Culler, *On Deconstruction,* p. 150.
30 See Alisdair MacIntyre, *After Virtue* (Notre Dame, Ind.: University of Notre Dame Press, 1984); Michael Sandel, *Liberalism and the Limits of Justice* (Cambridge: Cambridge University Press, 1982); Richard Rorty, *Philosophy and the*

language that could provide any ultimate support to the legitimacy of one mode of coordinating social life over any other. At this point, however, the communitarian antifoundationalist takes a direction different from that of the post-structuralist. The former, at least implicitly, admits the ultimate Nietzschean message of the presence of arbitrary will and radical contingency where once there were thought to be foundations. But he also quickly averts his attention, preferring instead to admire the peculiar coordinating force of language as it functions in a given social context. Caricaturing slightly: All contexts are fictions, but the ones in which we find ourselves embedded have a special legitimacy. For the post-structuralist, on the other hand, such an orientation, with its willful forgetting of will and contingency, allows us to settle too comfortably into the "soft collar" of our community's traditions.[31] When such appeals to the "soft" coordination by common meanings emerge, one can see in an especially clear way why there is a strong tie between the sense of responsibility to otherness and the world-disclosing capacity of language. Soft collars, in Foucault's hands, become garottes. With his metaphors from the world of punishment and warfare, he prys open soft, coordinating language and invites us to glimpse the world it proffers us in a radically different way.

In sum, post-structuralism is to be identified not just by its global statements that the linguistic coordination of action is based on fictions rather than foundations, but also by its concerted deployment of new fictions against whatever fictions are socially in force, however they happen to be justified (i.e., in either foundationalist or nonfoundationalist terms). Both of these tasks require a deep affirmation of the world-disclosing capacity of language, since it is the use of that capacity that can loosen our world's hold upon us by confronting us with the ways in which it is structured by unrecognized or willfully forgotten fictions. And as this hold is loosened, we become far more sensitized to the otherness that is engendered by those structures.

Taking stock now of what has emerged in this section, one can

Mirror of Nature (Princeton, N.J.: Princeton University Press, 1979). Rorty tries to distinguish himself from communitarians, but his unproblematic appeal to "our" values gives him some of the same problems they face. See Richard Bernstein, "One Step Forward, Two Steps Backward: Richard Rorty on Liberal Democracy and Philosophy," *Political Theory* 15 (November 1987), pp. 538–63.

31 Edmund Burke, *Reflections on the Revolution in France,* ed. with an introduction by J. G. A. Pocock (Indianapolis: Hackett, 1987), p. 67.

say that political reflection pursued under the pull of the responsibility to act in the world will generate cognitive machinery attuned to problems of action coordination; and, conversely, that political reflection pursued under the pull of the responsibility to otherness will use the world-disclosing capacity of language to loosen the hold of that machinery, as well as of the dominant modes of identity and action coordination connected with it. When the issue is stated in this way, one can see that there is what looks like an irrevocable tension between the two orientations. One can also understand why each orientation produces a specific recurrent critique of the other. The latter is charged with an irresponsible, apolitical aestheticism, as it plays with the world-disclosing capacity of language and shows us no theoretically informed way toward collective action; alternatively, it is charged with secretly desiring an aestheticized politics that exhibits a dangerous neglect of the distinction between, say, works of art and political action (a criticism often leveled at Nietzsche and Heidegger). On the other hand, political reflection pursued under the pull of a responsibility to act is charged with a conceptual imperialism that is blind to its harmful practical consequences.

IV. Between modernity and postmodernity

What is the status of the distinctions I have drawn? They are not intended to raise any strong metaphysical or ontological claims. However, they do have something like a quasi-ontological or substructural, interpretive status; that is, they reflect a reading of historical human being that, in turn, structures all of the other conceptualizations and interpretations one develops. This way of speaking is not meant to slip metaphysical privileges in the back door. What I mean can be clarified as follows: If, as suggested earlier, one follows postmoderns, like Foucault, to argue that all human constructs necessarily spawn otherness as an unavoidable effect, that claim *can* be understood as metaphysical or ontological. The world simply *is* that way. But it does not have to be, and should not be, understood in this fashion. Does this then mean that the claim is simply "more or less empirical"?[32] Yes, but there is a vast difference here between the "more" and the "less," as

32 Thomas McCarthy, review of Connolly, *Politics and Ambiguity*, in *Political Theory* 16 (May 1988), p. 343.

well as between the degrees of conviction that hang upon where a claim falls in this range. The assertion that human beings are never 3 inches tall is empirical, but less so than most assertions in social science. Many of our basic conceptions about human beings assume this assertion to be true. If it were false, we might be required to do some profound rethinking of human intersubjectivity. Foucault's assertion about otherness might be seen as less empirical in this sense.

A key ethical—political idea in modernity is that part of the responsibility to act includes the responsibility to take others into account. If we merely give the correct moral quality to our action, then others will be given their full due. Now we can interpret the history of Western civilization as exhibiting slow but persistent progress toward this goal. Such a basic, less empirical generalization then structures a variety of other, more specific interpretations of the present. And in relation to Foucault's claims about otherness, this generalization might lead us to believe that all his concerns could be met by merely heightening our present sensitivity. In other words, we do not need Foucault, just "a radicalized version of Mill's *On Liberty*."[33]

Foucault, however, has tapped a growing sense today that perhaps we ought *also* to read our history a different way, as warranting another (less empirical) generalization. We should indeed esteem steps in Western history like Mill's thought, but should we not also ask ourselves whether every such step included *as well* the sorts of problems to which Foucault attunes us? Just as Mill's aside about some people being more fit for despotism than free government makes us uneasy today, will our own contemporary, radicalized version of Mill not be read with similar feelings in the future?[34] My suggestion of thinking in terms of a noncollapsible distinction between a responsibility to act and a responsibility to otherness is intended to keep this dilemma in front of us and to explore what the effects of doing so might be on ethical and political reflection.

The distinction between the two functions of language ought to be taken in a similar way. It is not laid down in nature. Language that coordinates action can be analytically separated from world-disclosing language, but most usages are mixtures.

33 Ibid., p. 345.
34 John Stuart Mill, *On Liberty and Other Writings*, ed. by Stefan Collini (Cambridge: Cambridge University Press, 1989), pp. 13–14.

Very simple action-coordinating utterances may in fact involve significant slippages of meaning, just as world-disclosing utterances, such as a line of poetry, may in fact function to coordinate action. Of course, in practice we can always try to emphasize one dimension more than the other for particular purposes. Philosophically, however, it has been typical to try to emphasize one dimension by claiming for it some strongly privileged status. Habermas, following a tradition at least as old as Hobbes, has made the action-coordinating dimension predominant, just as Heidegger and Derrida have clearly done the reverse. My suggestion, on the contrary, is to give up such efforts and try to think about the implications of confronting both dimensions on something more like equal terms.

The distinction itself presses into consciousness as unbridled subjectivity is increasingly fixed upon as the key source of modernity's ills. The idea is that modern subjectivity's infinite urge to expand control over all aspects of life is strongly tied to a growing fixation on language as simply a means of action coordination. The reaction against this phenomenon emerges perhaps most clearly in Heidegger. When he claims that "We do not have language, rather language has us," he is trying to tell us that paying attention to the world-disclosing dimension of language is the first step toward relaxing this fixation and the infinite "will to planetary order" behind it.[35] It is the first step because the world-disclosing dimension is the one in which we must continually face our own finitude.

Heidegger's work is the best source to turn to in order to deepen the analysis of both of the distinctions I have introduced. There the side emphasized by post-structuralists and other postmodernists receives its most careful elaboration; and there, as well, emerge the dangers of a strategy of reacting to modernity's one-sidedness with an opposing one-sidedness.

35 Heidegger, *Hölderlins Hymnen "Germanien" und "Der Rhein,"* Vol. 39, *Gesamtausgabe* (Frankfurt: Klostermann, 1980), p. 23; and *Hölderlins Hymne "Der Ister,"* Vol. 53, *Gesamtausgabe* (Frankfurt: Klostermann, 1984), p. 59.

3

HEIDEGGER'S AMBIGUOUS LEGACY
FOR POSTMODERNISM

Heidegger is certainly one of the most troubling of all Western philosophers. In the same body of work we alternately find brilliant and beautiful insights and stupid and disgusting ones. It is no wonder that interpretations of him tend to extremes of praise and excoriation. My efforts in this chapter and the following one are premised on the conviction that we can adequately explore Heidegger's significance for postmodern reflection only if we do not forget either the heights or the depths of his thought. I develop a way of construing the latter in this chapter and the former in the following chapter.

Why turn to Heidegger at all? One might instead choose Nietzsche as the best source to investigate the roots of postmodernity. That strategy might have some advantages, but I prefer Heidegger for a couple of reasons. First, although he is indebted to Nietzsche in relation to his critique of metaphysics, he builds upon it in a way that feeds more directly into contemporary postmodern concerns; more particularly, he expands that critique into a critique of modernity's instrumental–technological orientation to the world, and he focuses more directly upon the nature of language. Second, I think there remains *some* truth in Heidegger's attack on Nietzsche's "will to power." It is often argued that Heidegger gives only a one-sided account of his forerunner. That is no doubt true.¹ Nevertheless, Heidegger at least calls our attention to how uncomfortably the problem of the will accords with other aspects of Nietzsche's thought. This more radical problematization of the will in the late Heidegger is significant for postmodern thinking, both for the positive insights it gives us and for the way it exposes how postmodern thinkers sometimes unconsciously encounter dilemmas similar to Nietzsche's. This difficulty can be seen, for example, in the frequent appeal to intellectual strategies of displacement, intervention, impertinence, explosive laughter – an armory of "spurs" to sink into the flanks of dominant discourses.² These strategies have a crucial role to play in postmodern political thinking; but unless they are located in a broader gesture of postmodern reflection, they threaten to resurrect, unconsciously, the specter of subjective will. The postmodern theorist who models his or her self-understanding *exclusively* on the role of ceaselessly exposing otherness slides all too easily into the position of the ring master of otherness.³

Heidegger, of course, has his own problems with the will, although they emerge in a different form. They manifest themselves most notably in his early thoughts about politics. The question of the fascist or authoritarian quality of Heidegger's work is an intensely debated one. Recent revelations about the depth of his association with Nazism have lent added weight to these charges.⁴ My primary concern here, however, does not depend

1 See the useful discussion of these issues in Fred R. Dallmayr, "Farewell to Metaphysics: Nietzsche," in *Critical Encounters* (Notre Dame, Ind.: University of Notre Dame Press, 1987), pp. 13–38; see Martin Seel, "Heidegger und Die Ethik des Spiels," in *Martin Heidegger: Innen- und Aussenansichten* (Frankfurt: Suhrkamp, 1989), pp. 136–59.
2 See Derrida, *Spurs: Nietzsche's Styles* (Chicago: University of Chicago Press, 1979). See Michael Shapiro's discussion of such strategies in "Weighing Anchor: Postmodern Journeys from the Lifeworld," in Stephen K. White, ed., *Lifeworld and Politics: Between Modernity and Postmodernity. Essays in Honor of Fred R. Dallmayr* (Notre Dame, Ind.: University of Notre Dame Press, 1989), pp. 139–65.
3 See the criticism of Derrida by Dallmayr in "Gadamer and Derrida," *Critical Encounters*, pp. 153–6.
4 The tide in this controversy has turned recently in a strongly negative direction. See especially Victor Farias, *Heidegger and Nazism*, trans. by Paul Burrell (Philadelphia: Temple University Press. 1989); Hugo Ott, *Martin Heidegger: Unterwegs zu einer Biographie* (Frankfurt: Campus, 1989); Jürgen Habermas, "Work and Weltanschauung," in *Critical Inquiry* 15 (Winter 1989), pp. 431–56; and Richard Wolin, *The Politics of Being: The Political Thought of Martin Heidegger, 1927–1966* (New York: Columbia University Press, 1990). Derrida's contribution to this controversy is contained in *Of Spirit*, trans. by G. Benning-

directly on such revelations. The concern is with a certain theoretical inadequacy in his thinking. Below the level of Heidegger's explicit political thinking is an inadequate conceptualization of action. More specifically, he never develops the conceptual resources that would have allowed him a satisfactory comprehension of the normative tension and interconnection between actors in social and political life. This flaw has two consequences. First, it helps explain why Heidegger could be so easily attracted to fascism in the 1930s, and why one is certainly justified in at least looking for the persistence of some form of authoritarianism throughout his work (Section I). But even if such suspicions prove not to be valid, the theoretical flaws in Heidegger's understanding of interaction and intersubjectivity are such that his thought cannot, by itself, ever form the basis of any adequate, nonauthoritarian approach to ethics and politics. The claim has recently been made that such an approach can be derived from Heidegger's later work and that it provides the best outline for postmodern political thinking. I argue that this claim cannot be sustained (Section II). It should be emphasized here that the underlying issue is the question of what theoretical resources are needed for an adequate model of postmodern politics. In defeating the claim that such a model can be drawn out of Heidegger's later work, one can learn something essential about the theoretical shoals on which thinking about postmodern politics typically runs aground.

This line of argument about Heidegger's inability to reconstruct adequately the responsibility to act is not intended to show that his thought is useless for addressing the postmodern problematic. I show in the following chapter how Heidegger's later work provides perhaps the best way of opening up the question of the responsibility to otherness.

I. Politics, will, and intersubjectivity

On the face of it, Heidegger's "A Dialogue on Language" seems to have nothing to say about ethics or politics. And yet,

ton and R. Bowlby (Chicago: University of Chicago Press, 1989). Derrida does not really try to defend Heidegger; rather, he seems to want to implicate metaphysical thought in general in the sorts of temptations to which Heidegger succumbed. See also Philippe Lacoue-Labarthe, *Heidegger, Art and Politics*, trans. by Chris Turner (Oxford: Basil Blackwell, 1990).

behind the beauty of this dialogue, one can sense what gets lost in Heidegger's thinking. The dialogue was occasioned by conversations between Heidegger and a Japanese professor, but the participants are curiously identified only as "a Japanese" and "an Inquirer."[5] The identities of both are thus almost completely washed away. In addition, there is the extraordinarily deferential attitude of the former to the latter. The stage directions, both explicit and implicit, for the conversation thus imply that the inquiry – "the matter of thought" [*Sache des Denkens*] – is more important than the participants.[6] The resulting tone of the dialogue is quintessential Heidegger: a reverential tarrying in the neighborhood of thinking and poetry. For the moment, I want to draw attention to only one thing about this tone: What it is an escape from. Heidegger always seeks to distance himself radically from the everyday clamor of contending voices.

Total attention to the inquiry, to the "matter of thought," is the only proper "response" [*Entsprechung*] of human being to the "*claim*" [*Anspruch*] of being.[7] Any emphasis on the participants in a dialogue, on anything like "the much-discussed I–Thou" relation, for example, merely reinflames that disease of subjectivity – calculating, claiming, and wanting – that is at the root of modernity's problems.[8] The thoughtless willing and wanting of everyday life is that from which essential thought must preserve itself. The clamor of the "they" [*das Man*], of "everydayness" [*Alltäglichkeit*], is the turgid water that Heidegger always fears will inundate his path. These voices are attuned to language only as a "means of trafficking," or a "tool" for mediating our claims and actions, not as the highest mode through which we participate in being. In everydayness, then, there resides the supreme threat of "forgetfulness" of being

5 "A Dialogue on Language," in *On the Way to Language*, trans. by Peter D. Hertz (New York: Harper and Row, 1971), p. 1. See also the roles of the participants in the dialogue "Conversation on a Country Path about Thinking," in *Discourse on Thinking*, trans. by J. M. Anderson and E. H. Freund (New York: Harper and Row, 1966), pp. 58–90.

6 "Letter on Humanism," in *Basic Writings*, ed. and introduced by David J. Krell (New York: Harper and Row, 1977), p. 241.

7 *Identity and Difference*, trans. and introduced by Joan Stambaugh (New York: Harper and Row, 1969), pp. 31, 94–5.

8 "Dialogue on Language," pp. 32–6.

and the essence of human being.[9] Thus Heidegger resolutely and consistently pushes the sphere of everyday, "face-to-face" [Gegen-einander-über] relationships out of his focus and holds fast to the exploration of that face-to-face relationship with "a more distant origin," the one with being.[10]

Heidegger's antipathy toward everydayness has been noticed, in a general way, by numerous commentators.[11] My specific concern with this antipathy is in how it condemns Heidegger to a lifelong misunderstanding of action. This misunderstanding may work its effect in different ways at different stages in his thought, but the distortion is never overcome. In his escape from everyday willing and wanting, Heidegger also necessarily takes leave of any possible adequate comprehension of the normative interconnection and tension between actors in social life.[12] By following this problem out, I am able to locate precisely the theoretical flaw in Heidegger as regards any possible practical implications; and this, in turn, contributes to locating correctly the value of his work for postmodern reflection.

The locus classicus of the charge that Heidegger's thought has a bent toward authoritarianism or fascism is his equation of the way

9 Being and Time, trans. by John Macquarrie and Edward Robinson (New York: Harper and Row, 1962), pp. 69, 149–50, 163–5; Hölderlins Hymnen "Germanien" and "Der Rhein," Gesamtausgabe, Band 39 (Frankfurt: Klostermann, 1980), pp. 22–3, 73; and Hölderlins Hymne "Andenken," Gesamtausgabe, Band 52 (Frankfurt: Klostermann, 1982), p. 10. In Being and Time, concepts like "everydayness" and "they" are of interest primarily for their inauthentic thoughtlessness. They do not yet have the specific negative historical meaning of unbounded calculating, willing, and wanting that Heidegger attaches to the everyday world and the "average man" as his sense of the crisis of modernity grows. See Allan Megill, Prophets of Extremity: Nietzsche, Heidegger, Foucault, Derrida (Berkeley: University of California Press, 1985), p. 126; and Heidegger's An Introduction to Metaphysics, trans. by Ralph Manheim (New Haven, Conn.: Yale University Press, 1959), p. 37.

10 "The Nature of Language," in On the Way to Language, pp. 103–4.

11 Recent ones include Michael Allen Gillespie, Hegel, Heidegger and the Ground of History (Chicago: University of Chicago Press, 1984), pp. 173–4; Megill, Prophets of Extremity, chs. 3 and 4; Winfried Franzen, "Die Sehnsucht nach Harte und Schwere," in Annemarie Gethman-Siefert and Otto Pöggler, eds., Heidegger und die praktische Philosophie (Frankfurt: Suhrkamp, 1988); and Jürgen Habermas, "Work and Weltanschaung."

12 My criticism of Heidegger on this issue will parallel Habermas's insofar as the latter condemns him for collapsing "all normative orientation into the power claims of a subjectivity crazed with self-aggrandizement" in The Philosophical Discourse of Modernity: Twelve Lectures, trans. by Frederick Lawrence (Cambridge, Mass.: MIT Press, 1987), pp. 134, 149. This parallel ends when Habermas develops his arguments into a near dismissal of Heidegger's later work.

both an art work and the work of a great political leader can open up a "world."[13] Each represents a supreme moment in which truth shines forth as a "strife" between "clearing and concealing." The opening of a world emerges out of the concealed "earth":

> As a world opens itself, it submits to the decision of an historical humanity the question of victory and defeat, blessing and curse, mastery and slavery. The dawning world brings out what is as yet undecided and measureless. . . .[14]

Now in one sense, Heidegger is making a correct point about the character of great political leadership: its creative setting into work of new historical directions for a people, and the dislocations and sometimes unavoidable violence that attend such a change. At such moments the population in a sense does have the character of material that is instrumentally molded. Heidegger, however, seems to inflate this sense into a model that neglects that this molding is always inextricably linked with preexisting networks of normative expectations. Great political leadership always has at least something to do with the way in which it brings into productive strive its formative efforts with the expectations of everyday life. The webs of such expectations sedimented, reproduced, and contested in practices and institutions constitute a middle dimension in political life between individuals and leaders.

Although *Being and Time* was not directed in any way toward political themes, its ontological starting point was such that it could not adequately conceptualize "intersubjective connectedness and obligation."[15] However much Heidegger may have departed in his later work from that origin, his antipathy for everydayness and what it embodies kept his theoretical concerns immunized from insights that might have led to a better understanding of this dimension. There is no doubt that Hei-

---

13 "The Origin of the Work of Art," in *Poetry, Language, Thought*, trans. and ed. by Alfred Hofstadter (New York: Harper and Row, 1971), p. 62; *Hölderlins Hymnen "Germanien" und "Der Rhein,"* pp. 120, 143–4; and *An Introduction to Metaphysics*, pp. 62, 191. See Alexander Schwan, *Politische Philosophie im Denken Heideggers* (Cologne: Westdeutscher Verlag, 1965).

14 "The Origin of the Work of Art," *Poetry, Language, Thought*, p. 63.

15 Carl Friedrich Gethmann, "Heideggers Konzeption des Handelns in *Sein und Zeit*," in *Heidegger und die praktische Philosophie*, p. 169. See Michael Theunissen, *The Other: Studies in the Social Ontology of Husserl, Heidegger, Sartre and Buber*, trans. by Christopher Macann, with an introduction by Fred R. Dallmayr (Cambridge, Mass.: 1984), ch. 5.

degger thought he was thematizing something like it with concepts such as people's "destiny" [*Schicksal*], "earth" [*Erde*], and "rootedness to the soil" [*Bodenständigkeit*].[16] These concepts might be understood as summing up all those qualities of situatedness and bindingness that characterize a community. Great political actions might then be thought of as being constrained by a middle dimension. In short, their greatness is measured not just by *creativeness* but by how such actions represent a *valid interpretation* of the normative webs that define a community. One senses here some notion of a horizontal dimension to political life where interpretations are contestable among participants of equal status.[17]

I do not wish to deny that there is this dimension in Heidegger. The problem, however, is that his concepts carry this horizontal quality in such a weak fashion that it is pulled asunder far too easily when subjected to the gravitational force of a more powerful figure of thought: That great action must free itself from the clamor and chatter of everyday contests of opinion and will. For this escape to be made good, political leadership cannot be subject to democratic influence. It is only when this is understood that one can fully make sense out of those chilling remarks Heidegger made during his short tenure as rector of the University of Freiburg in 1933–4. Any hint of a horizontal, interactive dimension to politics is swallowed up by the vertical dimension, a surrendering of individual will to that of the *Führer*.[18] Politics becomes primarily a matter of obedience to superior wills, not an accommodation reached between claims of equal status. The *Führer* may have to *interpret* the destiny of the *Volk*, but this interpretation is a matter beyond the willfulness of everyday politics; it cannot be forged in the sphere of the ordinary, only in the opening forced by extraordinary will.

Shortly after his resignation as rector, Heidegger began to

16 "The Self-Assertion of the German University," trans. by Karsten Harries, *Review of Metaphysics* 38 (March 1985), pp. 470–80; "The Origin of the Work of Art," *Poetry, Language, Thought,* p. 75; and "Memorial Address," *Discourse on Thinking,* p. 48.

17 This sort of interpretation of Heidegger is found in Karsten Harries, "Heidegger as a Political Thinker," *The Review of Metaphysics* 25 (June 1976), pp. 304–28.

18 The sort of interactive tension that Harries sees in the rector's speech between leaders and followers disappears when Heidegger tells students that "The *Führer* alone is the present and future German reality and law," in "German Students," *New German Critique* 45 (Fall 1988), p. 102.

distance himself a bit from the Nazis, but the attraction of this distorted image of political action, focused on the creative political will, clearly remained for a number of years.[19] This attraction appears to have subsided somewhat by the time of his lecture course on Hölderlin in 1942.[20] The precise cause of this shift is not made clear by Heidegger. But suddenly, political leaders are no longer included with "poets" and "thinkers" as creators. Perhaps the most plausible explanation is his growing concern about technologizing, calculative thinking.[21] Heidegger was progressively expanding his estimation of the depth and extent of this phenomenon in contemporary life.[22] Most likely this provided the motive for distancing himself both from Nietzsche and from the attraction of the world-disclosing acts of extraordinary political will. Both Nietzsche and great leaders now look less like solutions than new manifestations of the problem.

In the present context, the notion of technologizing, calculative thinking is crucial for several reasons. First, it functions as a model idea for radical postmodern thinking about our compulsively rational, "logocentric" orientation to the world. Heidegger exposes the grasping gesture of all "metaphysical" thought and shows how today each gesture has come to be embedded within a deeper gesture, placing everything into a "constituting" [Gestell] that lets us experience the world only as a standing reserve of potentially graspable stuff.[23] These images have had an im-

19 On the opening up of this distance, see Fred R. Dallmayr, "Heidegger, Hölderlin and Politics," Margins of Political Discourse (Albany, N.Y.: SUNY Press, 1989), pp. 207–20. But one should always be careful about overinterpreting scattered remarks critical of the Nazi regime as evidence that he had renounced fascism. If we follow Otto Pöggler's suggestion that Heidegger had always adhered to a somewhat idiosyncratic "Freiburger National Socialism," then it makes perfect sense for Heidegger to criticize specific aspects of Nazism while retaining a faith in fascism. See Pöggler, "Heideggers politisches Selbstverstandnis," Heidegger und die praktische Philosophie, p. 33.

20 Hölderlins Hymne "Der Ister," Gesamtausgabe, Band 53 (Frankfurt: Klostermann, 1984), pp. 44, 101–02. But even at this point, Heidegger retains other disreputable political traits, such as a crude nationalism; see pp. 68, 80.

21 See Harries, "Heidegger as a Political Thinker."

22 From Heidegger's perspective, Americanism, Bolshevism, and National Socialism are all dominated by the Gestell and thus are not in essence very different; see "Letter on Humanism," Basic Writings, pp. 220–1, and "Only a God Can Save Us," Spiegel interview, trans. by William J. Richardson in Thomas Sheehan, ed., Heidegger: The Man and the Thinker (Chicago: Precedent, 1981), pp. 55–6.

23 "The Question Concerning Technology," in Basic Writings, pp. 298ff. "Only a God Can Save Us," p. 58, translation altered; and "Überwindung der Metaphysik," Vorträge und Aufsätze (Pfüllingen: Neske, 1985), p. 75.

mensely powerful effect on the totalistic critique of reason pursued by postmodern thought. Likewise, the efforts in Heidegger's later work to "get over" [*verwinden*] the plague of such constituting create at least part of the basic horizon within which radical postmoderns seek what Heidegger calls "an other thinking" [*ein anderes Denken*].[24]

Heidegger's picture of a world driving toward an ever-greater rationalization of thought and action is also significant because, insofar as it offers us a picture of the social and political world, one sees that the earlier strife between the forgetfulness and clamor of everyday intersubjectivity and the opening provided by great acts of political will has revealed itself to be an inconspicuous mode of teamwork. They operate in tandem to fuel our blind, headlong dash toward an infinitude of certainty that will in fact bring only a certain finitude: planetary destruction. The world of Heideggerian political possibilities has thus gone from being two-dimensional to one-dimensional. Now all political acts and all political systems are conceptually leveled into so many moments of the intensification of our technological existence.[25]

As the image of the *Gestell* increasingly takes shape, so does Heidegger's awareness of the need for an "other thinking": a posturing of human being toward a "not wanting . . . beyond every type of willing." This is not, however, as is sometimes thought, a mystical appeal to a passive, meditative stance freed from all worldly stimulus. Heidegger emphasizes that such a posture overcomes the normal distinction of activity and passivity; it is "a higher form of doing than all acts in the world."[26] I have more to say later about how this is to be understood, especially as it relates to the intersubjectivity of everyday life. For the moment, however, it is essential to see only that, whatever concern for otherness means to Heidegger, it now cannot be willed into our consciousness and public life in any straightforward sense. To understand this is to understand how far Heidegger intended to distance his later work from anything that normally

---

24 "The Thing," *Poetry, Language, Thought*, p. 181; "Only a God Can Save Us," *Heidegger: The Man and the Thinker*, p. 58.
25 See the citations in n. 22.
26 "Conversation on a Country Path about Thinking," *Discourse on Thinking*, p. 61, translation altered. See *Gelassenheit*, 8th ed. (Tübingen: Neske, 1985), p. 33. On the differences between Heidegger's position here and a mystical orientation to the world, see Emil Kettering, *NÄHE: Das Denken Martin Heideggers* (Pfüllingen: Neske, 1987), pp. 250–2.

falls within the purview of practical philosophy, of any discussion of intersubjectivity and standards for action.

It is well known that Heidegger shied away from the task of developing an ethics.[27] The reason for this perhaps becomes clearer if one turns to a less well known but comparable declaration in regard to politics. Heidegger's early philosophical orientation to politics had focused on the acts of the leader, especially the idealized founding of the *polis* that opens a historical world. In the 1940s, one sees the same emphasis on the *polis* as opening, but now the focus of attention is its "pre-political [*Vor-politische*] essence" as an "open site" or "dwelling place" [*offene Stätte*] out of which political possibilities emerge.[28] There are certainly connections here with his earlier thinking, but decisive now is the separation of opening and will; political will is no longer part of the focus of attention, except negatively. The inference to be drawn from this is that political will and any philosophical attempts to evaluate it entangle themselves necessarily in the *Gestell*. And it is this same fear that motivates Heidegger's distancing of himself from ethics.[29]

Heidegger maintained this conviction to the end of his life, eschewing any attempt to formulate systematic proposals about ethics or politics. Critics who remain suspicious of the political implications of Heidegger's work often tend to interpret his writings from the 1950s on as a mode of "mysticism" that merely overlays the persistence of authoritarianism.[30] Evidence of this is seen both in the disturbing but unsystematic remarks Heidegger made in an interview published after his death (e.g., his questioning whether democracy could meet the challenge of the *Gestell*) and in what he failed to take responsibility for in his own Nazi past.[31] But these doubts are also often connected to the identification of recurring figures of thought that appear to many to carry a systematic bent toward authoritarianism.

---

27 "Letter on Humanism," *Basic Writings*, pp. 231ff.
28 *Hölderlins Hymne "Der Ister,"* pp. 44, 101–2.
29 This argument is made in regard to ethics by Gerald Prauss, "Heidegger und die Praktische Philosophie," in *Heidegger und die praktische Philosophie*, pp. 186–8.
30 See Habermas, *The Philosophical Discourse of Modernity*, p. 137; and Megill, *Prophets of Extremity*, p. 146.
31 See Habermas, *The Philosophical Discourse of Modernity*, pp. 155–6; Megill, *Prophets of Extremity*, p. 146; and George Steiner, *Heidegger* (New York: Penguin, 1978), p. 123.

There are three such figures of thought. First is the totalistic, one-dimensional quality of the crisis of modernity; all distinctions between existing political systems are declared trivial. Second, there is the assertion that we cannot, in any direct sense, do anything to alleviate this crisis. Efforts toward resolution mean a mere reigniting of the will. This figure of thought was even supplemented, at least some of the time, by the idea that being has "withdrawn" from the world; thus any clear path out of our crisis is most surely cut off. The most we can do is adopt a posture of "waiting."[32] Finally, there is a continual appeal to the possibility that in time we will be saved from crisis. But, again, we cannot will a hastening of "that which will come" [*das Kommende*], the coming turn in the "history of being" [*Seinsgeschichte*].[33]

It has been argued that these figures of thought add up politically to a "diffuse readiness to obey," an "empty readiness for subjugation."[34] But this judgment seems a bit too eager to find a necessary latent authoritarianism. The three figures of thought might more likely lead to a thorough uncooperativeness with anything political. But I am not so much interested in trying to claim this as in suggesting that no *adequate* approach to ethics or politics could possibly come out of such a position. The reason is simply that from within Heidegger's categorical framework, an ethics or politics simply cannot emerge. To the degree that Heidegger implies that part of the sense of *das Kommende* is a radically new politics, he not only forgets his own self-declared limits, he also commits a category mistake. He blunders thereby from his powerful ontological insights about a nongrasping posture of allowing things to *come into presence* into a speculative reference to the *coming of a historical occurrence*. The former can, as I show, be reconstructed as a way of answering the sense of responsibility to otherness. The latter, however, can only be thought about in terms of action concepts that Heidegger spent his life avoiding thinking about. Anything that could qualify as a

---

32 "Building, Dwelling, Thinking," *Basic Writings*, p. 328; *Nietzsche*, Vol. IV, *Nihilism*, trans. by F. A. Capuzzi and ed. by D. F. Krell (New York: Harper and Row, 1982), pp. 238–50; *Hölderlins Hymne "Der Ister,"* p. 165; "Conversation on a Country Path about Thinking," *Discourse on Thinking*, pp. 62ff.

33 *Hölderlins Hymnen "Germanien" und "Der Rhein,"* pp. 97, 146; *Hölderlins Hymne "Der Ister,"* p. 165; "Hölderlin and the Essence of Poetry," in *Existence and Being*, trans. and introduced by W. Brock (Chicago: Regnery, 1949), p. 289; and "Only a God Can Save Us," *Heidegger: The Man and the Thinker*, p. 57.

34 Habermas, *Philosophical Discourse of Modernity*, pp. 140–1.

better political world would have to be describable in terms of practices and institutions; and to speak that language is to speak about how actions might be coordinated – how the tensions between claims and wills would be related to structures of normative expectation.

Heidegger's hyperbolization of modernity's dilemma may have a certain kind of validity for postmodern reflection, as it seeks to highlight the dangers of rationalizing the world. Such hyperbole functions as an unsettling intervention into the smooth operation of the modern mind. But insofar as this mode of thinking is joined with the vague and seductive hope that somehow the world can experience "a change from the ground up,"[35] Heidegger at best offers confusion and at worst a disdain for small, democratic politics.

II. Heidegger and a postmodern politics

Negative judgments about Heidegger's implications for ethics and politics have not gone unchallenged. Reiner Schürmann in particular has joined an analysis of the later work with the claim that we can derive from it a nonauthoritarian orientation for praxis. Although others have tentatively explored this direction, Schürmann is worth examining in detail because of his extraordinary boldness in pursuing such an interpretation.[36] By attending closely to his arguments, I hope to achieve two things. First, his incisive reading of the later work is helpful in laying the basis for what I want to say about Heidegger and the responsibility to otherness in the next chapter. Second, in showing the error of his claims about a Heideggerian orientation for politics, one learns something in general about the postmodern difficulty with handling the responsibility to act.

Critics of Heidegger's politics tend to focus on the early work

35 Pöggler, "Heideggers politisches Selbstverständnis," *Heidegger und die praktische Philosophie*, p. 54.
36 Reiner Schürmann, *Heidegger on Being and Acting: From Principles to Anarchy*, trans. by Christine-Marie Gros (Bloomington: Indiana University Press, 1987). For another, more cautious attempt to win some nonauthoritarian orientations for ethics and politics from Heidegger, see Fred Dallmayr, "Ontology of Freedom: Heidegger and Political Philosophy," *Political Theory* 12 (May 1984), pp. 204–34; *The Twilight of Subjectivity: Contributions to a Post-Individualist Theory of Politics* (Amherst: University of Massachusetts Press, 1981), pp. 64–71; and the essay cited in n. 19.

and then search through the husk of the later so-called mystical work for the kernels of persisting authoritarianism. Schürmann, on the contrary, focuses first on the later work, trying to demonstrate its coherence. Then, reading backward, he finds that Heidegger's early explicit authoritarianism disappears completely and that even those later figures of thought that others have found disturbing can be reinterpreted in a clearly nonauthoritarian fashion. Ultimately, Schürmann is more interested in the guiding force that Heidegger's later work ought to have for us than he is in whether Heidegger's own judgments about history and politics fully accommodated themselves to this guidance. He is aware that, at some points, his reading may lead "in a direction the man Martin Heidegger would not have wished to be led."[37] From my perspective, this is a perfectly legitimate approach, since what is at issue are figures of thought and the conceptual options they open or close for postmodern thought.

> If we ground ourselves in Heidegger's later work, the practical implications of his thinking leap into view: the play of a flux in practice, without stabilization and presumably carried to the point of an incessant fluctuation in institutions, is an end in itself. . . . [This] reveals the essence of praxis: exchange deprived of principle.[38]

Schürmann characterizes this new approach as "anarchic praxis."[39] But he also makes clear that what he intends with this concept is not directly related to traditional anarchist political theory, with its models of new societies without a state. The term here refers to a broader, more radical suggestion about how action in general must be understood, once we accept Heidegger's arguments that our prevailing thinking about action condemns us to a compulsive reiteration of the *Gestell*. The whole of Heidegger's deconstruction of metaphysical reason from Plato to the present is intended to get us to think about action differently. We must abandon the picture of action as grounded in and continually guided by a metaphysical *archē*. Once Heidegger, following Nietzsche, deconstructs the conventional character of all "principial economies" within the history

37 Schürmann, *Heidegger on Being and Acting*, pp. 3, 293.
38 Ibid., p. 18.
39 Ibid., p. 293.

of Western civilization, we are faced with the realization that action is "bereft of arche" or principle: "in its essence, action proves to be an-archic."[40]

Up to this point, such a reading of Heidegger dovetails effortlessly with contemporary postmodern thinking. But Schürmann also wants to distinguish Heidegger from much of French deconstruction precisely in how his thinking about action goes beyond it. This distinction emerges once we appreciate how the later Heidegger "radicalized" the ontological difference into "the *temporal difference*."[41] The key ideas here are "origin" and "originary," "history" and *Ereignis* (or "appropriating event"). "Origin" has the meaning of the inception of a historical "economy of presence" that can be analyzed and deconstructed as a unity related to some *archē*. Such an economy would have something like the character of those *epistemes* that are a central focus of Foucault's interest. But Heidegger wants to think of difference not only as the difference between "historical orders of *presence*," but also of the difference between all such unities, on the one hand, and the uncentered, manifold presenc*ing* that holds across historical time, on the other. The sense of Heidegger's *Ereignis* is here interpreted as that "event-like distributing of presence-absence" that is the "a-priori" of any possible economy of presence.[42]

This reading of the relation of *Ereignis* and history allows Schürmann to show that it is incorrect to see Heidegger simply as a forerunner of postmodern deconstruction. Across the discontinuities of historical epochs, Heidegger reads a continuity of presencing: "a force of plurification and dissolution."[43] The whole sense of his "other thinking" is to bring about a kind of face-to-faceness with such presencing. Although Schürmann does not make this point, I argue later that this peculiar face-to-faceness is one of the key components that makes Heidegger's reconstruction of the responsibility to otherness so powerful. And it is the lack of such a moment in much of contemporary French thinking that limits the horizon of its reconstruction. Having said this, however, it is important to emphasize that Schürmann's interpretation does not by any means divorce Heidegger from historical, deconstructive concerns. These concerns

40 Ibid., pp. 4, 84, my emphasis.
41 Ibid., pp. 145ff.
42 Ibid., pp. 74, 144–5, 283.
43 Ibid., pp. 12, 127.

are essential, and Schürmann criticizes those who find in the later Heidegger nothing but an ahistorical, face-to-face posture toward *Ereignis,* that is, who read Heidegger as the pure rhapsodist of "the Poem of Being." One must see that the cogency of Heidegger's claims about *Ereignis* or presencing depends upon its being understood in relation to the deconstruction of the "history of being," of the different historical "economies" of presence.[44] This is the case because, although we always already have immediate access to presencing, that access is always momentary and deeply colored by the prevailing economy of presence. The full sense and significance of "originary" presencing can thus be won only by attending to how it differs from, and is continuous through, the "origins" of such economies. The implication is that "being can only be retrieved indirectly."[45]

Schürmann thus attempts to show how Heidegger's attention to the "temporal difference" allows him to develop formal categories that give coherence to the notion of presencing. These categories delineate how, over against the unifying modes of historical presence, presen*cing* is utterly plural, unstable, motile, and unhierarchial. They allow us "to elaborate the chief traits of an economy of *presencing* that is not reducible to one *archē*" – the traits of a "plural" or "postmodern" economy.[46]

In relation to the question of action, the most immediately important category related to presencing is "*Gelassenheit*": "releasement" or "letting be." *Gelassenheit* is offered as the proper response of human being to the ontological condition of presencing. It manifests "compliance with presencing," a posture that releases itself from the compulsive reiteration of the *Gestell.*[47] In order to understand how this concept links up with a postmodern politics, however, one must first understand how the realm of present historical possibility appears from the perspective of what Schürmann calls Heidegger's "hypothesis of closure." This is the idea that we may now be on the threshold of a "transitional" era brought to birth by the extremity of the *Gestell* in our lives and the beginning of a "withering away of faith in principles" that could possibly preside over some new, unitary economy of presence. With this "turning" [*Kehre*], there emerges the possibility of a

44 Ibid., p. 127.
45 Ibid., pp. 157–8
46 Ibid., pp. 12–13, 45, 157–8, 206.
47 Ibid., p. 35.

categorically different economy: a new "opening" in which "words, things and deeds find their site."[48]

Again retaining the focus on action, several claims are associated with this hypothesis. First of all, Schürmann wants to interpret the "political domain" as precisely this opening or site in which "words, things and deeds come into a definite historical arrangement."[49] This, as I showed earlier, is the way Heidegger thinks of the *polis* in his later work. Heidegger, however, is a bit more careful, speaking not in sweeping terms of *the* political but rather of the "prepolitical essence of the polis." Schürmann's slippage here is symptomatic of the growing difficulties that he encounters as he focuses more precisely on the concepts of action and politics.

This broad sense of the political as opening or site must, of course, be supplemented by a narrower one referring to possible practices within a constituted public sphere, that is, a sphere of activity reconstructed upon that site. What is distinctive about the opening our transitional era confronts us with today is that it can become the basis of a "postmodern economy" of words, things, and deeds – and thus ultimately an "other" politics.[50] The radical distinctiveness of this politics versus all hitherto existing forms is grounded in the changed meaning action would have.

When Heidegger spoke of *Gelassenheit* as an orientation that overcomes the normal dichotomies of activity and passivity, doing and thinking, his intention was to indicate a "broader concept" of action than that which has dominated Western thought since Aristotle. This latter "restricted concept" has always envisioned action as being guided by reason (in the sense that reason represents a goal for it) and sustained by the will. For Heidegger, this narrow, essentially teleocratic conception of Aristotle is already on its way toward the *Gestell*, within which action is identified with the production of effects guided by strategic reason. Teleocratic action is thus part of the "essence of technology" that today bears its ripe fruit: technological society and technocratic politics.[51]

48 Ibid., pp. 1, 74, 78–85.
49 Ibid., pp. 84–5.
50 Ibid., pp. 242, 293.
51 Ibid., pp. 82–4. See Heidegger, "The Question Concerning Technology," in *Basic Writings*, p. 309. This effort at a one-dimensionalization of Aristotle and contemporary strategic, technocratic views of action and politics would be questioned by many; see especially Brian Fay, *Social Theory and Political Praxis* (London: Allen and Unwin, 1975).

The broader nonteleocratic conception of action, *Gelassenheit,* is intended to emphasize the limits of the narrower one and thus to demarcate the space for a new praxis, opening now in our transitional condition. *Gelassenheit* is not a praxis that is assigned a goal by thinking or theory. Rather, to learn "other thinking" means first practicing an attitude or posture of human being toward being or presencing. It is an orientation that "complies" with the character of presencing as plural, unstable, motile, and unhierarchial. Moreover, this posture is inherently political in the broad sense: It both constitutes an *intervention* in our teleocratic, technocratic disposition over words, deeds, and things, and it *prepares the site* for – but cannot directly will – a new, postmodern, anarchic disposition within which an other politics can emerge.

This two-sided quality of *Gelassenheit* embodies the theme of mortality or finitude that was always so essential to Heidegger. To practice *Gelassenheit* is to practice a "politics of 'mortals'," as opposed to a politics of the " 'rational animal'."[52] The latter finds its extreme limit in the desperate drives to infinities of knowledge, control, and security. On the one hand, *Gelassenheit* would mean intervening in this drive and deflating its claims and the urge to infinitude. This side of *Gelassenheit* would seem to be appropriately manifested in the strategies recommended by poststructuralists like Foucault and Derrida. The other side of *Gelassenheit,* though, refers to developing a face-to-faceness with presencing that somehow lets things be in their particularity, that lets us exist finitely alongside them. This direction is only sketched by Heidegger, and he continually emphasizes the merely preparatory and anticipatory quality of his suggestions. Thus, the second side of *Gelassenheit* must be seen as opening itself, on the one hand, to a radically different "other thinking" and an "other" politics corresponding to it but, on the other hand, not claiming to embody them fully. Such other being in its *full* sense would "have left behind" today's "Janus-like ambiguities . . . and would have turned Proteus-like."[53]

In situating *Gelassenheit* on the border of an "other" politics, Schürmann seems to be trying to bring into sharper focus some possible practical sense of *das Kommende.* My problem with the

---

52 Schürmann, *Heidegger on Being and Acting,* pp. 154, 281.
53 Ibid., pp. 229, 242.

picture he has drawn is that the "other" politics remains an empty category. By this I do not mean that it is simply utopian in the sense of "nowhere present," but that it is literally nonconceivable, given Heidegger's conceptions of action. Here one begins to suspect that Schürmann has not succeeded in bringing Heidegger out of the dilemma highlighted at the end of the previous section. But by his efforts to push the Heideggerian project further – and in nonauthoritarian directions – he both allows one to see the heart of this dilemma more clearly and helps thereby to unearth some of the deep difficulties that contemporary postmoderns have with political reflection.

Why exactly is an other politics nonconceivable? Schürmann and Heidegger would, of course, not want it to be conceivable in technocratic, *Gestell*-contaminated terms. That means it must be somehow conceivable as emerging out of the two-dimensional orientation of *Gelassenheit*. Somehow it "would arise" out of this "anarchic praxis."[54] Part of what is perplexing here lies in the idea that this practice does not achieve its effects by a frontal assault of the will, but rather obliquely. Now there is nothing mysterious or wrong per se with this sort of figure of thought in political reflection. It is often appealed to, for example, in scenarios of nonviolent civil disobedience, where one does not expect the disobedience to force a regime directly to take an action, but rather to have a subtle effect on public opinion that, in turn, would call into question the legitimacy of some policies of that regime. But within the Heideggerian framework, this figure of thought seems to have the latent function of deflecting attention from a deep conceptual gap between *Gelassenheit* and any possible "other" politics, between action heightening our sense of the broader meaning of *the* political (or prepolitical essence of the *polis*) and a narrower sense involving ongoing, everyday patterns of involvement in the public sphere.[55]

The anarchic praxis of *Gelassenheit* is radically separated from any discourse about the legitimation of public actions.[56] For to talk the language of legitimacy – as postmoderns also incessantly warn us – is to reinscribe our thinking in the *Gestell*, to bring it back within the domain of "principial" regimes. But it is precisely here that one begins to feel the deeply debilitating effect of the

54 Ibid., pp. 242, 293.
55 Ibid., p. 293.
56 Ibid., pp. 89ff.

one-dimensionalization that is at the heart of Heidegger's concept of *Gestell*, as well as the analogous way in which many postmoderns think about logocentrism, metanarratives, and societal rationalization. One-dimensionalization here has the effect of disallowing a foregrounding of any sense of legitimacy that could cut against a technocratic world and provide at least some procedural, conceptual bridge toward an "other" politics.

But why is such a bridge necessary? It is necessary – conceptually necessary – because politics involves collective action; and unless such action is to be reduced to coordination purely through threats and incentives, it must be conceived as somehow built up out of courses of interaction in which claims are raised and agents held responsible to normative expectations, which are themselves not immune from reflective scrutiny. And this complex of interaction – what Habermas calls "communicative action" – cannot plausibly be scrubbed free of the associated concepts of rightness, justice, or legitimacy. The problem here is that Heideggerian thinking about action, caught between the sole alternatives of *Gestell* and *Gelassenheit*, is simply unable to make this "world" of collective action "arise" into view.

No matter how we work with the notion of *Gelassenheit*, it will not by itself yield up the interactional, normative dimension of politics. Insofar as one side of this concept falls together with contemporary deconstructive or genealogical strategies, it suffers the same fate as they do when it comes to understanding this dimension. As critics have often pointed out, the distancing, defamiliarizing gesture of these strategies, with their aim of exposing the effects of power and rationalization in our normative conversations, comes at the cost of losing any resources for thinking back to what better conversation might resemble.[57] The second side of *Gelassenheit*, the sense of somehow complying with presencing and thereby bearing witness to finitude, can, I think, become just such a resource, as I try to show in the next chapter; but it has to be correctly understood, and that means not seeing it as an orientation out of which a new politics imminently blossoms. In explicating this side of *Gelassenheit*, Schürmann quotes Heidegger: "In the most hidden ground of his essence, man is like the rose – without why," that is, without goals for his action

57 See Charles Taylor, "Foucault on Freedom and Truth," *Political Theory* 12 (May 1984), pp. 152–3.

or the compulsion to legitimize it.[58] From this goalless posture *alone,* this deep suspension of the responsibility to act, the way toward any possible modes of collective action will always remain a mystery.

Why did Heidegger never comprehend the gap? As suggested in the previous section, his mandarin antipathy toward everyday life kept his theoretical focus of attention removed from where it would have to be in order to understand the conceptual basis for such a gap. But Schürmann has no such antipathy, and he is committed to reading Heidegger in a way that not only overcomes the gap but also points us toward a predilection for small, radical democratic politics. This same predilection is evident in most contemporary postmodern thinkers. Thus something more generally useful may be learned from following Schürmann's attempt to coax Heidegger over the gap.

At the heart of Heidegger's work is an explicit vision of the essence of language and human being. In the work of postmodern thinkers there is nothing so explicit. But there is at least a subtle privileging of certain similar qualities of language and human being that follow from the strong sense of answering the responsibility to otherness they share with Heidegger. In particular, they privilege notions such as plurality, difference, motility, instability, dissemination, and lack of hierarchy. Schürmann and other postmoderns are also irresistibly drawn to the idea that these categories and those of radical democracy have some strong affinity. The two sets simply seem to be, in some loose way, homologous.[59] Of course, these thinkers sharply reject the idea of a derivation of the validity of democracy from ontological categories, for that would smack too much of modern ways of relating thought and action, theory and practice.

I showed in the last chapter that the theoretical stance of Foucault and Derrida always draws them toward a gesture of withholding when it comes to a systematic discourse on politics. And yet, in practice, both have been associated with activities that would fall under the rubric of small, radical democratic politics.[60] Moreover Foucault, when pushed, admitted that, although all politics involves disciplinary forms, "consensual disciplines" are

58 Schürmann, *Heidegger on Being and Acting*, p. 38.
59 Ibid., pp. 279–81.
60 See Keith Gandal, "Foucault: Intellectual Work and Politics," *Telos* no. 67 (Spring 1986), pp. 121–34.

better than nonconsensual ones.[61] However problematic this phrase is from within his own theoretical perspective, it suggests the desire to align that perspective *somehow* with the small democratic politics he supported in practice. The same is true of his suggestion that his thinking might be of value to new social movements.[62] Other postmoderns, like Lyotard, also have this distinct bent.[63] Thus, there is a rather strong implication that postmodern reflection somehow disposes us in this practical direction.[64]

Again, the root of this disposition seems to be the way radical democracy reflects the central categories of the responsibility to otherness. This mirroring effect makes it appear that postmodern thinking opens naturally toward small, radical democracy, but in such a way that it does not become entangled within new discourses about legitimacy or justice. The problem, in Schürmann's Heideggerian terms, is to have a politics attuned to presencing and yet not initiate a new principial regime.

By following Schürmann, one can understand precisely why this way toward political thinking is flawed. There may be affinities between the Heideggerian-postmodern vision of language and human being (from which those key categories of difference, plurality, etc. arise), on the one hand, and a certain image of politics, on the other. But these affinities remain too weak unless they are mediated by a different complex of concepts.

Schürmann argues that once we have understood Heidegger's temporal difference, we must also accept that "in its essence" action is "bereft of *archē*." And if we understand radical democ-

---

61 Foucault, "Politics and Ethics: An Interview," in P. Rabinow, ed., *The Foucault Reader* (New York: Pantheon Books, 1984), pp. 378–80.

62 Foucault, "On the Genealogy of Ethics," *The Foucault Reader*, p. 343; and "Two Lectures" in *Power/Knowledge: Selected Interviews and Other Writings 1972–1977* (New York: Pantheon Books, 1980), pp. 80–1.

63 Lyotard, *The Postmodern Condition*, pp. 60–7; Lyotard and Jean-Louis Thébaud, *Just Gaming*, trans. by Wlad Godzich with an Afterword by Samuel Weber (Minneapolis: University of Minnesota Press, 1985), pp. 87ff.

64 A striking exception to this tendency is Richard Rorty. He would argue that postmodern reflection should not necessarily dispose us to any particular political forms. In a Burkean manner, he simply chooses to stick with the tradition – the "We" – into which he was born: North American democracy. See "The Priority of Democracy over Philosophy," in M. Peterson and R. Vaughan, eds., *The Virginia Statutes of Religious Freedom* (Cambridge: Cambridge University Press, 1988). A good critique of this position is contained in Richard Bernstein, "One Step Forward, Two Steps Backward: Richard Rorty on Liberal Democracy and Philosophy," *Political Theory* 15 (November 1987), pp. 538–63.

racy correctly, we will understand it as manifesting the "absence of any principle of legitimation." This form of politics thus allows action to become free in the sense of attaining its essence.[65] Schürmann's interpretation of radical democracy is based on a curious use of Hannah Arendt's reflections in *On Revolution*.[66] There she focused on the radical forms of democracy that emerged for brief moments in various revolutions from the eighteenth to the twentieth century. In each instance, there was an attempt to free the public domain from the coercive weight of the previously dominant principles and institutions. This, Schürmann suggests, prefigured a Heideggerian desire to release ourselves from the compulsive need for a public life securely grounded in first principles.[67] Laws lose their permanent mooring in a principial regime; they arise rather from permanently renewed deliberation that carries with it a consciousness of the conventionality, fallibility, precariousness, and revisability of all political arrangements. This kind of consciousness thus stays close to the Heideggerian essence of the political (in the broad sense): an opening for realigning words, things, and deeds. Insofar as radical democratic practices allow such an opening to occur consistently, they reflect those basic categories of presencing: difference, plurality, and so on.

This sense of radical democracy is extraordinarily important to emphasize today, as ossifying rationalization processes expand in Western societies. But it can take on a distorted significance when it is torn away from another sense: that of acting with the *goal* of mutually generating and maintaining legitimate procedures for keeping politics open. Action in this sense can only be conceptualized within some framework that captures both a moment of teleology and a moment of mutual, dialogical responsibility. Neither Heidegger nor contemporary postmoderns can thematize this complex because they have at their disposal only two ways of thinking about action: the condemned teleological modes spawned within the *Gestell*, or the countermodes that have no goal, no "why," or at least none other than that of unmasking metanarratives and rationalization processes.

This point is often glossed over by postmoderns. From Schürmann's efforts, one can see not only why this glossing has an

---

65 Schürmann, *Heidegger on Being and Acting*, p. 91.
66 Hannah Arendt, *On Revolution* (New York: Viking Press, 1965).
67 Schürmann, *Heidegger on Being and Acting*, pp. 91, 290.

initial plausibility, but also why it is ultimately rather deceptive. There is nothing wrong with describing radical democracy as essentially tied to the absence of *final* goals. But there is a real difference between this and the further implication that such a politics – thought of now as something like an "other politics" – has, as its guiding spirit, action without *any* goal, without any "why."

4

HEIDEGGER AND RESPONSIBILITY
TO OTHERNESS

So far I have shown how Heideggerian concepts are inadequate for expressing the full sense of a responsibility to act and thus for giving adequate guidance to ethical and political reflection. I want to reverse my direction of analysis now and draw out the rich sensitivity Heidegger had for the responsibility to otherness. My ultimate goal is to elaborate this sense of responsibility in such a way that one will see why it cannot simply be subsumed under the responsibility to act. If this is true, it means that ethical and political reflection will, in some way, have to define itself into a relationship with the responsibility to otherness.

The notion of otherness is introduced by way of a discussion of finitude (Section I). Then I present a more detailed analysis of how Heidegger proposes that we experience otherness, drawing out especially an important difference from the leading French postmoderns (Section II). In the following chapter, I develop the foregoing themes in a more direct engagement with these contemporary thinkers.

I. Finitude and action

The spirit of the last chapter can fairly be called Habermasian, since I was using his conception of communicative action as the most adequate way of reconstructing the essential ideas cohering around the responsibility to act. But the critical force of this spirit, which is so effective initially, grinds to a halt at a certain point. And that is the point at which it is appropriate to begin to reconsider Heidegger.

Habermas is not only deeply suspicious of the direct practical implications of Heidegger. He, like many others, also finds the later work to be a melange of confused ideas that claim for themselves a special status beyond all reason and argumentation. And to make matters worse, despite all of the mystical acrobatics of other thinking, in the end it lands us right back on the ground of a philosophy of consciousness, of the *subject* standing *cognitively* over against being.[1] With this conclusion, I would suggest that reflection pursued under the responsibility to act has begun to stumble badly. Perhaps the best way to see this is to return briefly to Habermas's early conception of "knowledge-constitutive interests."[2] I am, of course, aware that he no longer considers this to be an adequate basis for the theory of communicative action.[3] But the point I am going to make is, I think, still valid.

What interested Habermas is how modes of knowledge take the form they do because they correspond to anthropologically deep-seated interests of the human species. These interests were identified as "technical," "practical," and "emancipatory."[4] Now I am not directly interested in the fact that Habermas's framework was criticized as a species of philosophical foundationalism, that is, as having claimed to provide a final or ahistorical ground on which human being is clarified. What interests me is that all of the three interests he delineated fall within the sway of the sense of responsibility to act; they refer to different moments of that responsibility. One way in which the validity of this characterization becomes clear is if the question is raised: Why is there no knowledge-constitutive interest in death? The meaning of this question would be: Why is what counts as knowledge not in some way responsive to the interest in making sense of our lives being

1 Habermas, *The Philosophical Discourse of Modernity: Twelve Lectures*, trans. by Frederick Lawrence (Cambridge, Mass.: MIT Press, 1987), pp. 136–9, 151.
2 Habermas, *Knowledge and Human Interests* (Boston: Beacon Press, 1971).
3 Habermas, *The Theory of Communicative Action*, Vol. 1, *Reason and the Rationalization of Action* (Boston: Beacon Press, 1984), preface.
4 Habermas, *Knowledge and Human Interests*, pp. 175–6, 196–8, 308ff.

finite? Within Habermas's framework we are creatures who seek to manipulate things in the world, to understand one another, and to get out from under domination, but we are not creatures who die. Once seen, this hole in the framework appears vast and unmanageable. It will not do to try to force the fact of our finitude under one of the existing interests. The practical interest in understanding would be the likely candidate, but finitude is not *simply* another subject about which we seek understanding. Alternatively, it is not very illuminating either to try to work up a new, separate cognitive interest to which, say, religion specifically answers. To understand the significance of the question I have raised, one has to see it as changing the tone of all of Habermas's interests. Each of the three is a project of human being; but to proceed as Habermas does is to try to conceive of those projects while forgetting finitude. And to do that is in effect to essentialize human being under the sway of the responsibility to act.

After this basic choice has been made by Habermas, it is not surprising that his comprehension of Heidegger's project is so unsatisfying. Habermas no doubt thinks it ironic that Heidegger ends up in the same cognitive–technical sphere as modes of thought that reflect the *Gestell*. But I would suggest that what is in evidence here is simply a fundamental misunderstanding.

It has been argued that all of Heidegger's work tends toward one central concern: remembering the finitude of being.[5] In *Being and Time*, the analysis focuses specifically on individual *Dasein* and death.[6] The everyday world of thought and action holds our attention in a way that makes us forget our finitude. But that finitude cannot always be kept submerged; it reemerges suddenly and in ways we cannot control. We become gripped by "anxiety" [*Angst*] about our own death, a mood that overcomes us and within which the hold of all our projects seems to give way to the flood waters of nothingness. The proper response to finitude is for *Dasein* to confront it and learn to will itself resolutely.

In the later work, however, this sort of quasi-heroic picture largely dissolves and is replaced by a much more subtle set of sketches suggesting what it would mean to posture ourselves in a

---

5 Dennis Schmidt, *The Ubiquity of the Finite: Hegel, Heidegger and the Entitlements of Philosophy* (Cambridge, Mass.: MIT Press, 1988), p. 24.

6 *Being and Time*, trans. by John Macquarrie and Edward Robinson (New York: Harper and Row, 1962), pp. 274–311.

way that quietly let the "ubiquity of the finite" into life.[7] It is only within this horizon that one can understand Heidegger's ideas about being and language.

One of Heidegger's favorite lines from Hölderlin's poetry is: "Full of merit, and yet poetically dwells Man on this earth."[8] Here Heidegger evokes that pair of distinctions to which I have been continually returning. There is, on the one hand, all that "man works at and pursues" and thereby earns or "merits'; all that is pulled within the wake of the responsibility to act, and sustained and coordinated "within everyday language." In the English translation, the "and yet" that follows "Full of merit" signals the divide, but its signal is a pale reflection of the starker, more forceful negation of the German "*doch.*" Heidegger sees a "sharp opposition" at the divide, for the world of merit "*does not touch the essence of his* [man's] *sojourn* on this earth."[9] And that essence is our "dwelling poetically." Human being has the capacity for poetry, which in its essence is "the granting [*Stiftung*] of being by means of the word." And it is only by attending to this capacity that we are "touched by the nearness of the essence of things."[10] And that essence, as Heidegger comes to see more and more, has to do with finitude: coming into presence, passing into absence.

The two senses of language and responsibility are evoked here quite elegantly.[11] However, with his continual use of "essence," Heidegger leaves no doubt as to which sense is to be given priority. The one is the "real" [*Wirkliche*], the other the "unreal" [*Unwirkliche*].[12] In this unblushing straightforwardness, Heidegger distinguishes himself from his contemporary postmodern progeny. They shun such a direct stance, preferring instead to unmask the attempts to essentialize human being in relation to the responsibility to act. They thereby leave a more indirect suggestion. Whether direct or indirect, however, the effect of such

---

7 This phrase comes from the title of Dennis Schmidt's book cited in n. 5.
8 See "Hölderlin and the Essence of Poetry" in *Existence and Being,* introduced by W. Brock (Chicago: Regnery, 1948), p. 282.
9 Ibid.
10 Ibid; translation slightly altered.
11 Of course, it must be remembered that, at the time Heidegger wrote this essay, such thoughts were still linked with disturbing political implications.
12 *Hölderlins Hymnen "Germanien" und "Der Rhein," Gesamtausgabe,* Band 39 (Frankfurt: Klostermann, 1980), p. 217. See "Hölderlin and the Essence of Poetry," p. 276.

essentialization is to obscure the possible linkage of their best insights to ethics and politics.

What makes Heidegger's directness particularly interesting is the intensity of focus it brings to his later work. There is literally no other theme than that of exploring how we should respond to otherness. My intention in this chapter is to try to begin to appropriate some of Heidegger's insights here without taking in tow either his one-sided privileging of the responsibility to otherness and world-disclosive language or the pernicious images of politics to which he always remained attracted.

With this clarification of overall aims, let me return to the connection of finitude and "dwelling poetically." In another discussion of Hölderlin's poetry that dates from the same period as the one referred to earlier (1934–6), Heidegger discusses the meaning of community [*Gemeinschaft*] in relation to mortality. What he has to say is undeniably still bound up with his deeply disturbing political views, but – *looking backward now*, as Schürmann suggests – there are other things going on as well. Most important, he suggests that it is only within the "space" of a genuine community that we "can hear one another" [*Voneinander-Horenkonnen*]. But the space for such an "originary community" [*ursprungliche Gemeinschaft*] is not generated by "the taking up of a mutual relation" mediated by language functioning as a "means of understanding" [*Verständigungsmittel*]. It is generated only by a "nearness [*Nähe*] of death," as in the case of "soldiers at the front." This nearness alone can bring us to a posture in which our everyday chatter of willing and wanting subsides and we really become open to hearing one another.[13]

Now as I indicated, this discussion is easily linked to political will, resoluteness, and readiness to sacrifice for the German people, the result of which is a pernicious set of political images. But there are other dimensions of meaning in these remarks about community that point toward themes in the later work. In the last chapter, I emphasized Heidegger's notion of the prepolitical essence of the *polis* largely in terms of its negative significance, as indicating a retreat from thinking about politics in terms of great acts of will. The positive significance was elucidated only as calling attention to that *opening*, to which all normal politics is related as a *closing* down of the parameters of thought and action.

13 Ibid., pp. 72–3.

This rather vague reference to opening can now be given a more definite sense.

At first, the experience of finitude would appear to issue in an understanding of closure rather than openness. And yet Heidegger suggests just the opposite. To confront our finitude is to confront a closure *beyond our will*. And to confront that is to begin to feel the precariousness of all our *willed* closures. Those willed closures thereby start to lose that sense of the potential for infinite mastery that they take on when we are under the exclusive sway of the responsibility to act. And it is only as that certainty begins to ebb that we really become open to hearing one another. What Heidegger is implying here is that the genuineness of a community rests upon a radical willingness to hear and experience the difference of the other. Heidegger's later work is adequately comprehended only when one understands it as so many attempts to think through this experience and willingness.

Putting Heidegger together in this way glosses over, however, a persistent difficulty. The discussion of community I have referred to is quite atypical. Heidegger seldomly speaks of intersubjective otherness; and when he does, this form of otherness and human relationship is usually heavily subordinated to the question of otherness as it emerges within the question of being.[14] I have already examined some of the reasons for this bent, as well as some of its deleterious consequences. But what I want to suggest now is that even though this is true, one may still draw upon Heidegger's insights in ways that can be made fruitful for ethics and politics.

A moment ago, I suggested one shift in the way the later Heidegger differs from the earlier when considering finitude. It is the shift from a quasi-heroic struggle with to a humble affirmation of mortality. This change intersects another that expands the question of finitude from the individual to the social–historical level. This is the level on which it must be asked: What do we do now that our religious and metaphysical anchors are giving way and everyday life is dominated by the ersatz infinity of a "will to will"? The two levels of finitude cannot, of course, be

---

14 See the discussion of love in "What Is Metaphysics?" in *Basic Writings*, ed. and introduced by David J. Krell (New York: Harper and Row, 1970), pp. 101–2; "What Are Poets for?" in *Poetry, Language, Thought*, trans. and ed. by Alfred Hofstadter (New York: Harper and Row, 1971), pp. 127–8; "Andenken," in *Erläuterungen zu Hölderlins Dichtung*, 5th ed. (Frankfurt; Klostermann, 1981), pp. 142ff; and the discussion of friendship, also in "Andenken," pp. 127ff.

divorced; but on the social–historical level the questions become more complicated, because they must be answered in ways that are more historically mediated and directly related to collective practice. As Schürmann rightly points out, Heidegger's other thinking is not just a set of timeless directions for personal attunement to the Poem of Being. Another way of putting this is to stress that what Heidegger is grappling with is the possibility of a collective learning process in regard to finitude that makes sense only for us as historical beings.

This is important to emphasize because, however much Heidegger seems to delineate other thinking in contrast to reason, it remains a thinking about the "unlearning" processes of modernity: an increasingly one-sided cognitive–instrumental orientation to the world expressing itself in the pressures for societal rationalization. The challenge Heidegger presents us is not that of a total rejection of modernity but a rebalancing of it: a relearning of our finitude.[15] But what exactly does "learning" mean in this sense? Perhaps this can be made a bit clearer by again playing what is at issue off against Habermas. He has provided what is arguably one of the most powerful narratives we have about the learning processes of modernity. Moreover, he gives us some useful ways of beginning to think simultaneously about our unlearning process – that same one-sidedness Heidegger assails.[16] But from *within* an intellectual project pursued exclusively under the sway of the responsibility to act (and thus with no appreciation of finitude), Habermas cannot fully come to terms with this unlearning. Learning about our unlearning, keeping ourselves postured so as to be sensitive to all its dimensions, is not something for which reason, in its Habermasian reconstruction, gives us sufficient resources. For Habermas, we learn only insofar as we can bind ourselves to "rationalization complexes" in which there is "an accumulation of knowledge."[17] But the sort of learning toward which Heidegger wants to turn us is not cumulative. It may "gather" in some sense, but it is "a becoming aware that gathers, that remains a listening"; or a kind of remembering, a "recollecting" [*Andenken*] of all that is shoved aside and forgotten

15 See Habermas's criticism of Heidegger in *Philosophical Discourse of Modernity*, ch. 6.
16 Habermas, *The Theory of Communicative Action*, Vol. 2, *Lifeworld and System: A Critique of Functionalist Reason* (Boston: Beacon Press, 1987), p. 400. See my discussion of this theme in *The Recent Work of Jürgen Habermas* (Cambridge: Cambridge University Press, 1988), pp. 133ff.
17 Habermas, *The Theory of Communicative Action*, Vol. 1, pp. 237–8.

in modern consciousness.[18] But, again, it is not a total rejection of reason, a leap into irrational mysticism or pure aestheticism. One does not climb into the warm womb of Being or become the play of presencing and absencing. Learning the "other" remains reflexive.

This last fact is probably expressed best in the metaphor Heidegger uses in his introduction to the collection of essays he wrote on Hölderlin's poetry. For Heidegger, Hölderlin's poems come closer to the direct expression of *Ereignis* than any others. But other thinking is not such pure expression; it is a mode of reflection in which we try to learn a new way of orienting ourselves to finitude or otherness. Heidegger cites the following lines from Hölderlin:

> Because of lesser things
> Muffled as by snow was
> The Bell, with which
> One calls to supper.[19]

Referring to his own efforts to elaborate Hölderlin's poems, he suggests that "Perhaps every elucidation of these poems is a snowfall on the bell."[20] The reflective distance here is from poetry. But one should also understand "bell" here on a deeper level as meaning being or *Ereignis*. And, with that reading, thinking is distanced even further.

What then is this orientation that is not pure attunement, but rather always recognizes that it "muffles" the sound of otherness? Heidegger speaks of it as a kind of "responding" [*Entsprechen*].[21] In the terms in which I have been speaking, it is a way of taking up the responsibility to otherness. Responsibility in this sense has a rather different meaning than in the sense of responsibility to act.[22] In the latter domain, our action and reflection

---

18 " '. . . Poetically Man Dwells . . .'," *Poetry, Language, Thought*, p. 223; translation slightly altered.

19 Cited by Heidegger in "Vorwart zur zweiten Auflage," *Erläuterungen zu Hölderlins Dichtung*, p. 7.

20 Ibid., pp. 7–8.

21 "Language," *Poetry, Language, Thought*, p. 209; *Identity and Difference*, trans. and introduced by Joan Stambaugh (New York: Harper and Row, 1969), p. 31.

22 See Reiner Schürmann, *Heidegger on Being and Acting: From Principles to Anarchy*, trans. by Christine-Marie Gros (Bloomington: Indiana University Press, 1987), pp. 260ff.

are bound up with giving an account or reckoning before various courts of rational appeal. This is the domain of responsibility from whose closure not only Heidegger but also contemporary postmodern thought wants to flee. Foucault expresses it succinctly when he speaks of the " 'blackmail' of the Enlightenment" and the police mentality that is always demanding "to see that our papers are in order."[23]

But what does it mean to appeal to responsibility in a radically different sense? For Heidegger, this appeal grows out of the necessity of responding to *Ereignis,* presencing-absencing, finitude.

II. Other thinking

Perhaps the most famous line in Heidegger comes from his *Der Spiegel* interview in 1966, where he asserted that our current crisis is so bad that "Only a god can save us."[24] This is Heidegger at his worst: the old, essentially unrepentent, Nazi donning the mantle of a prophet of doom. On the basis of what I argued in the preceding chapter, perhaps the best way to understand this proclamation is as the only thing he *could* possibly say about our collective future, given both his desire for change from the ground up and his failure to articulate any concepts in terms of which collective action might be envisioned. Here one finds nothing but a dead end for thought.

Heidegger, however, followed this famous remark with another, which refers us to a different, richer strain in his thinking. He tells us that we must hold ourselves open for the arrival *"or* for the absence of a god in our destruction."[25] The contrasting of "destruction" and "saving" is simple enough (and just as uninteresting philosophically). But the notion of openness to the absence of a god is not immediately intelligible. What I want to suggest in the following is a way of interpreting this notion originally picked up from Hölderlin. It is slowly molded by Heidegger until it blossoms into what is distinctive about other thinking.

Hölderlin's poetry is deeply bound up with the experience of

23 "What Is Enlightenment?" in *The Foucault Reader,* ed. by Paul Rabinow (New York: Pantheon, 1984), pp. 42–3; and *The Archaeology of Knowledge,* trans. by A. M. Sheridan Smith (New York: Harper and Row, 1972), p. 17.

24 "Only a God Can Save Us," *Spiegel* interview, trans. by William J. Richardson in Thomas Sheehan, ed., *Heidegger: The Man and the Thinker* (Chicago: Precedent, 1981), p. 57.

25 Ibid., pp. 57–8; translation slightly modified; my emphasis.

the "flight of the gods." His dwelling upon and elaboration of this experience became an almost inexhaustible source for Heidegger, who returned to it again and again. In Hölderlin the experience of absence remains oriented toward the possible coming of new gods. In Heidegger, however, this familiar figure of thought undergoes a curious slippage. Although he continues to speak of a possible coming of new gods, it has an increasingly strange sound when placed within the full context of his later thought.

A moment ago, I suggested that from the perspective of the inadequate conceptualization of action in his early work, Heidegger's appeal to "saving gods" seems a lot like a deus ex machina. The plot itself is not rich enough to provide the resources for a satisfactory resolution of the play. The gods are therefore crucial. But if one considers this appeal within the context of the other thinking in his later work, a rather different feeling emerges. The appeal still sounds like a deus ex machina, only now an additional plot has surfaced with enough richness that the coming of the gods seems strangely unnecessary.

What gives rise to this situation is that, in Heidegger's hands, the experience of absence, finitude, that which is beyond the self's grasp – otherness – is slowly built up into a mode of posturing human being, in relation to which "coming gods" has a rather archaic ring. In other words, the experience itself takes on a self-sustaining coherence and is no longer tuned primarily by the expectation of a new coming. In his monological dialogue about *Gelassenheit,* Heidegger expresses the heart of this idea. Other thinking, one of the characters says, means "Waiting [*Warten*] . . . but never expecting [*erwarten*]." Another character answers, "The waiting has essentially no object."[26]

In what follows, I sketch out how Heidegger conceives this new posturing of human being toward absence, finitude, otherness. Before doing this, however, it is essential to say something briefly about how Heidegger's efforts have often been misunderstood by contemporary postmoderns. In the last chapter, I mentioned that the posture Heidegger wanted to elaborate had an

26 *Gelassenheit,* 8th ed. (Tübingen: Neske, 1985), p. 42. See the English translation in "Conversation on a Country Path," *Discourse on Thinking,* trans. by J. M. Anderson and E. H. Freund (New York: Harper and Row, 1966), p. 68. At other times, Heidegger, despite his own warning, uses *erwarten* to characterize the attitude of waiting; see "Building Dwelling Thinking," *Basic Writings,* p. 328. For the German, see *Vorträge und Aufsätze* (Pfüllingen: Neske, 1985), p. 145.

unusual face-to-face quality. I am going to suggest, finally, that it is this quality that keeps other thinking from sliding into that reinflated figure of subjectivity that dogs postmodern thinking: the ring master of otherness.

For postmoderns, the idea of any sort of face-to faceness reeks of the worst sorts of concepts associated with metaphysical, logocentric modes of thought. It is no accident that Foucault and Derrida have followed Nietzsche in this. Foucault encourages "the explosion of man's face in laughter"; and Derrida succinctly informs us why this is imperative: "The face is presence, *ousia*."[27] For all his admiration of Heidegger, Derrida has always seen him as too deeply wedded to "an entire metaphorics of proximity, of simple and immediate presence, a metaphorics associating the proximity of Being with the values of neighboring, shelter, house, service, guard, voice and listening." We end up, says Derrida, wrapped in "the security of the near," folded safely back into a new metaphysical blanket.[28]

Derrida is wrong here, and his failure makes it difficult to see the real distinctiveness of Heidegger. The latter wants to elucidate a sense of face-to-face experience, but not one that slides into all the old metaphysical traps. Derrida, however, sees him as simply wanting to distance himself from the *Gestell* by edging into the "nearness" [*Nähe*] of being. *Nähe* is indeed a counterconcept to *Gestell*, but Derrida fails to understand what is at issue.[29] The one-dimensional image of humanity nearing being radically misconstrues *Nähe*. From the lectures on Hölderlin to the end of his life, Heidegger emphasized the complex and non-one-dimensionality of *Nähe*. He refers to a "refusing-withholding nearness" [*verweigernd-vorenthaltenden Nähe*]. Similarly, he speaks of "being at home" [*Heimischsein*] as "the becoming at home in not being home" [*das Heimischwerden in Unheimischsein*].[30] Clearly, something

27 Foucault, *The Order of Things: An Archaeology of the Human Sciences* (New York: Random House, 1970), pp. 385–6; and Derrida, "Violence and Metaphysics," in *Writing and Difference*, trans. and introduced by Alan Bass (Chicago: University of Chicago Press, 1978), pp. 101, 142–3. In this essay, Derrida expresses more sympathy for the idea of face-to-faceness than in the later essay, "The Ends of Man," in *Margins*, trans. by Alan Bass (Chicago: University of Chicago Press, 1982), where there is deep suspicion of any such idea.
28 "The Ends of Man," pp. 130, 133.
29 See Emile Kettering, *NÄHE: Das Denken Martin Heideggers* (Pfüllingen: Neske, 1987), p. 17.
30 "Time and Being," in *On Time and Being*, trans. by Joan Stambaugh (New York: Harper and Row, 1972), pp. 15–16; translation altered. *Hölderlins Hyme*

more is going on here than the elaboration of a simple "meta-phorics of proximity." Heidegger is trying to sketch the contours of a mode or modes of experience that have a face-to-face quality inadequately appreciated by contemporary postmoderns. At the same time, however, this quality is not captured adequately within the sort of account someone like Habermas gives of a face-to-face, performative attitude among actors taken as claimants. The latter attitude is taken up within the pull of the responsibility to act. Heidegger's distinctiveness resides in his attempt to think out a face-to-faceness that answers to the responsibility to otherness.

In his first lectures on Hölderlin in 1934, one sees the initial sketch of this new posturing. Heidegger interprets Hölderlin as helping us toward the only adequate way to experience the flight of the gods. We must learn to posture ourselves so that we re-main open to that which is beyond our mortality, but we must simultaneously renounce [*verzichten*] the urge to name it, either in the form of disinterring old gods or of setting up new ones. It is only in the *distance* [*Ferne*] maintained by this renunciation or relinquishing that *nearness* to "godliness" [*Göttlichkeit*] is pre-served.[31] For my purposes, what is important to see in this early discussion are three things. First, nearness is not thought of in simple opposition to distance; rather, the two somehow sustain one another in the experience Heidegger wishes to explore. Sec-ond, it is not difficult to see how Heidegger becomes increasingly fascinated by the idea of such an experience or posturing as a counter to *Gestell*, in which, he says, we remain blind to our finitude and obsessed with overcoming all distances and drawing everything within the nearness of our potential grasp.[32] Third, what Heidegger here calls "godliness" is later replaced with the more familiar Heideggerian concepts of the "holy" [*Heilige*] or the "clearing" [*Lichtung*] of being.[33]

What exactly does Heidegger intend with his concept of *Nähe*?

"Der Ister," *Gesamtausgabe*, Band 53 (Frankfurt: Klostermann, 1984), pp. 147, 159, 173. In fairness to Derrida, it should be mentioned that when he wrote his essay, neither of the texts I just quoted may have been available to him. But the idea is expressed in earlier texts as well; see *Erläuterungen zu Hölderlins Dichtung*, p. 24.

31 *Hölderlins Hymnen "Germanien" und "Der Rhein,"* pp. 81, 94–5.
32 See "The Nature of Language," in *On the Way to Language*, trans. by Peter D. Hertz (New York: Harper and Row, 1971), pp. 102ff; and "The Thing," in *Poetry, Language, Thought, pp. 165–6*.
33 See Kettering, *NÄHE*, pp. 197–8.

He wants to delineate a way of experiencing otherness such that it remains other, a mode of posturing the self that "lets the other be" in its difference. Understood in this sense, *Nähe* has a complexity to it that goes beyond its ordinary meaning of simple nearness.[34] The complex Heideggerian notion connotes something more like a neighborhood or space of experience within which things are "measured" differently than within the space of *Gestell*. Within the latter, getting nearer implies a better grasp of something, potentially better control. Within the former, near and far do not function simply as spatial opposites, but rather as two sides of a playing back and forth in relation to the other. Attentive concern for otherness means that the gesture of nearing, bringing into one's presence, into one's world, must always be complemented by a letting go, an allowance of distance, a letting be in absence, thus bearing witness to our own limits, our own finitude. For Heidegger this is a "movement" [*Bewegung*] that is also a "way-giving" [*Be-wegung*] in the sense of an orienting of our experience.[35]

In order to understand the structure of the experience of *Nähe*, it is helpful to turn to what Heidegger says about the essence of language: that world-disclosing quality that emerges most clearly in poetry. Great poetry, for Heidegger, is measured by its capacity to open up *Nähe*.[36] Such poetry cannot be adequately understood with the model of artistic expression, that is, as containing images that are simply an expression of the artist's imagination. Heidegger's alternative model is perhaps most clearly expressed in his essay "Language," where he discusses Georg Trakl's poem "A Winter Evening," the first stanza of which reads:

> Window with falling snow is arrayed
> Long tolls the vesper bell
> The house is provided well,
> The table is for many laid.

If the speaking here is not simply expression, what is it?

34 Ibid., pp. 17–18 (esp. n. 9). For Kettering, *Nähe* is not only a key concept in Heidegger, it is *the* key concept.
35 This sense is lost in the existing English translation. See "The Nature of Language," in *On the Way to Language*, pp. 102–4; and "Das Wesen der Sprache," in *Unterwegs zur Sprache* (Pfüllingen: Neske, 1986), pp. 209–11.
36 Kettering, *NÄHE*, p. 193.

The speaking names the winter evening time. What is this naming? Does it merely deck out the imaginable familiar objects and events – snow, bell, window, falling, ringing – with words of a language? No. This naming does not hand out titles, it does not apply terms, but it calls into the word. The naming calls. Calling brings closer what it calls. However this bringing closer does not fetch what is called only in order to set it down in closest proximity to what is present, to find a place for it there.

To find a "place" in this sense would mean to place something before us [*vorstellen*] in order to put ourselves in a position to close down parameters and act. In such naming or calling, language is functioning as a potential coordinator for action.

> The calling here calls into a nearness. But even so the call does not wrest what it calls away from the remoteness, in which it is kept by the calling there. The calling calls into itself and therefore always here and there – here into presence, there into absence. Snowfall and tolling of vesper bell are spoken to us here and now in the poem. They are present in the call. Yet they in no way fall among the things present here and now in this lecture hall. . . .
>
> > The house is provided well,
> > The table is for many laid.
>
> The two verses speak like plain statements, as though they were noting something present. The emphatic "is" sounds that way. Nevertheless, it speaks in the mode of calling. The verses bring the well-provided house and the ready table into that presence that is turned toward something absent. What does the first stanza call? It calls things, bids them come. Where? Not to be present among things present; it does not bid the table named in the poem to be present here among the rows of seats where you are sitting. The place of arrival which is also called in the calling is a presence sheltered in absence. The naming call bids things to come into such an arrival.[37]

Again, Heidegger wants to consider how we can call or name things in a way that is not merely the first step toward fulfilling the responsibility to act. Our *creative* bringing into presence in language must be joined with a *preserving* of the sense of otherness or absence out of which that presence appears and to which

37 "Language," *Poetry, Language, Thought*, pp. 198–9.

it must finally be let go. To take up this posture to otherness or absence is to sense the way in which our world of action must be taken as fragile and finite – just the opposite of what we are given to think in the attitude of the *Gestell.* Such a posture thus expresses our finitude, responds to otherness.[38] And, in so doing, it also participates in that originary process of *Ereignis* in a way only human beings can, given their capacity for language.

It is according to this sketch of experience that Heidegger continually sought to draw out the idea of an other thinking and *Gelassenheit.*[39] Here it is not a question of everyone trying to become a poet, but of fostering a particular type of "thinking experience" that he often referred to as "recollection" [*Andenken*].[40] Although Heidegger first uses this idea in relation to how we should orient ourselves to the gods who have fled, it comes to be synonymous with other thinking. This emerges most clearly in the essay on "The Thing." There Heidegger presents one of his most well-known efforts to show how one fosters a thinking experience with the world that is different from experiencing it in the attitude of the *Gestell.*[41] As with the discussion of poetry I have touched upon, his thoughts on how to experience things in the world are guided by his notion of *Nähe.*

One helpful way of opening up the sense of *Andenken* and *Nähe* is in terms of the moods [*Stimmungen*] appropriate to them. In *Being and Time*, as I mentioned earlier, the mood associated with the experience of finitude is anxiety. Its message of finitude has an unalloyed, piercing quality that must be answered by individual resolution. *Angst* does not disappear in Heidegger's later work, but its role seems to change. It becomes important as that "helpless anxiety" [*ratlos Angst*] that "we" of the atomic age feel under the ever-present threat of nuclear death and the living nightmare of an ever-expanding urge to "planetary domination."[42] The onset of such a mood, however, is no longer ade-

---

38 Heidegger plays on the sense in which experiencing things [*Dinge*] in this way shows us our condition [*Bedingung*] as mortals [*Sterblichen*]: "Die Dinge bedingen die Sterblichen"; "Die Sprache," in *Unterwegs zur Sprache*, p. 22. See the English version, "Language," in *Poetry, Language, Thought*, p. 200.
39 See "The Nature of Language," in *On the Way to Language*, pp. 101ff.
40 *Erläuterungen zu Hölderlins Dichtung*, pp. 30, 153.
41 "The Thing," in *Poetry, Language, Thought*, p. 181. But the terminological continuities are lost in the English translation; see "Das Ding" in *Vorträge und Aufsätze*, esp. p. 174. See also *Erläuterungen zu Hölderlins Dichtung*, p. 153.
42 "The Thing," p. 166; "Das Ding," p. 158.

quately responded to by individual resolution. Although the threat is still unalterably personal, Heidegger is now emphasizing its collective dimension: The roots of nuclear death and planetary domination are in that common attitude of the *Gestell*. Anxiety now is, at best, a mood that starts us on a long process of realizing how deep the problem of adequately responding to finitude lays. The emergence of this realization and the learning of such an orientation are accompanied by moods rather different from anxiety. The moods that tune *Nähe* do not have the unalloyed quality of anxiety. Rather, they carry within them an indissoluble ambiguity. This ambiguity mirrors the playing back and forth of nearness and distance, presence and absence, as well as the idea that we must learn to be at home in homelessness. Heidegger speaks both of a "grieving joy" [*trauernde Freude*] and of "shyness" or "awe" [*Scheu*].[43]

In both moods there is a current of attraction, fascination, and delight balanced by a current of reticence, sobriety, respect, or mourning. One way of construing what Heidegger might have been intending here can be illuminated by a comparison with the more accessible example of Thoreau's *Walden*. That book simultaneously evokes both the intense delight of the continual, always surprising, and diverse presencing of things; and a poignant, mournful sense of their fragility, singularity, and momentary quality.[44] Moreover, Thoreau, like Heidegger, is perplexed by the question of "dwelling" or building a life in which such experience is kept alive.[45] But for both Thoreau and Heidegger, the vividness and place of *this* experience of everydayness is persistently shunted aside by the bustle and self-enclosure of what comes to define our modern everydayness. I would suggest that the concept of *Nähe* can be understood as aimed at opening up or vivifying this submerged potential for experiencing everydayness.

If Heidegger is interpreted in this way, then some of the more questionable concepts of his later work might be given more interesting and plausible readings. *Das Kommende* especially might take

---

43 *Erläuterungen zu Hölderlins Dichtung*, pp. 27, 77, 131–2, 161.
44 See Stanley Cavell's thoughts on the "everyday" in Thoreau and Heidegger, in particular his suggestion that *Walden* puns continually on the delight of "morning" and the grieving of "mourning," in "The Uncanniness of the Ordinary," in Sterling M. McMurrin, ed., *The Tanner Lectures on Human Values*, Vol. VIII (Salt Lake City: University of Utah Press, 1988), p. 108.
45 See "Building Dwelling Thinking," as well as the idea of "ethos" in "Letter on Humanism," in *Basic Writings*, pp. 231ff.

on a different sense. It would no longer be that conceptual monstrosity that refers us to some mysterious, overpowering, collective future in which gods or Being "decide" to emerge out of their
withdrawnness. Rather, it could be taken as expressing hope that
fostering a different sort of experience might begin to work its
effects on our modern lives. One can now better understand the
sense in which I earlier raised the issue of a subtle learning process
that is also an unlearning process. We would be unlearning that
compulsion to infinitude that tunes the *Gestell*. It is clear that
Heidegger's concept of the *Gestell* is overly one-dimensional, but if
we focus on the compulsion to infinitude, the essential value of his
insight is highlighted. This compulsion accompanies, like a
shadow, the responsibility to act and the action-coordinating function of language.

The learning implied here is a learning to answer the responsibility to otherness more effectively. But, as I suggested earlier,
there is a strong asymmetry between learning in this sense and
learning under the sway of the responsibility to act. Habermas
may be right when he emphasizes that the distinctive cognitive
attitudes of modernity are the only ones that allow knowledge to
accumulate.[46] And this distinction should be taken as indicating
that modern structures of consciousness deserve a certain privileged status over against premodern structures. But the acceptance of this point should not be taken to establish the additional
claim that there is no learning at all if it is not describable as
accumulative in a strong sense. Most would agree that one can
learn something that is not purely personal or idiosyncratic by
reading or watching the performance of a great tragic work. But
it would be missing the point to describe what was learned in
accumulative terms: as if one should see as many tragedies as
possible in order to construct a list of situations one should avoid
at all costs. Perhaps then it makes some sense to see in the fostering of a counterexperience like *Nähe* something describable as
learning.[47]

Another concept that takes on a more intriguing sense when
viewed in relation to the underlying idea of such counterexperience is the "fourfold" [*das Geviert*] of "earth," "sky," "mortals,"
and "gods."[48] The proper way of experiencing things, says

46 Habermas, *The Theory of Communicative Action*, Vol. 1, pp. 236–9.
47 See Cavell, "The Uncanniness of the Ordinary," pp. 109ff.
48 "The Thing," in *Poetry, Language, Thought*, pp. 177ff.

Heidegger, is to locate them in the play of these four dimensions of "world." Taken literally, the fourfold would seem to yield sense only as some positive, mystical, or religious doctrine. As such, this concept would sit uncomfortably with most of the other concepts of Heidegger's later work. Perhaps, however, we should interpret things a little less literally here, somewhat the way one does with Rousseau's attempt to illustrate the general will with a mathematical formula.[49] Proceeding in this way, *das Geviert* then can be seen as *one* attempt to illustrate the interplay of the themes I have emphasized: presencing-absencing and finitude.[50]

If one reconstructs the drift of Heidegger's later work as I have in this chapter, then one has a way of understanding the deep connections between Heidegger and postmodern thought as well as a crucial difference. In regard to the latter point, I have tried to show how Heidegger constructs a response to otherness that takes the form of resettling everyday life with a new mode of experience. One *faces* the world differently. This distinguishes Heidegger from contemporary postmoderns who emphasize, as it were, the slapping of faces, laughter in faces, an impertinence before the unity and simple presence faces traditionally claim to embody. My purpose in dwelling on this difference is to suggest that an *over*emphasis on disruption and impertinence creates for postmodern thinking a momentum that threatens to enervate the sense of responsibility to otherness, subtly substituting for it an implicit celebration of the impertinent subject who shows his or her virtuosity in deconstructing whatever unity comes along. The result is an ironic one for postmodernism's own self-understanding. Moreover, this momentum allows postmodern thought to become an easy target for its many critics who assail its irresponsibility and destructive tone. What I am suggesting is that this momentum must always be held in check by postmodernism's continually returning to its best impulses. The strategies of deconstruction, genealogy, and so on must continually reaffirm their rootedness

---

49 Jean-Jacques Rousseau, *The Social Contract and Discourses*, trans. and introduced by G. D. H. Cole (London: J. M. Dent, 1973), p. 185.

50 See *Erläuterungen zu Hölderlins Dichtung*, p. 153. For all the differences in their interpretations of Heidegger, Schürmann and Kettering largely agree on not taking *das Geviert* as some positive doctrine; Kettering, *NÄHE*, p. 381; Schürmann, *Heidegger on Being and Action*, pp. 222–5. However, Schürmann tries to put substantial distance between the concepts of *Nähe* and *das Geviert*. I find no justification for this in Heidegger's texts (especially "The Thing").

in the responsibility to otherness; and the later Heidegger's explication of that sense in terms of finitude is unequaled.

Earlier I spoke of the sense of responsibility to otherness as a moral–aesthetic sense. When the momentum of impertinence dominates, the moral dimension suffers and postmodern thinking opens itself to the charge of mere aestheticism.[51] The promise of Heidegger's later work resides ultimately in its hints about how to situate ourselves in the seam between the aesthetic and the moral. The seam is the other thinking into which flow both experiences with the world-disclosing or poetic dimension of language and the concern with finitude. The way in which Heidegger's work opens out into the moral dimension is, however, immensely problematic. What I have offered in the preceding discussion is a way of getting at Heidegger's well-known distinction between what normally passes for morality or ethics, on the one hand, and something more "essential" ("ethos" or "dwelling"), on the other.[52] I have tried to bring out the sense of these latter concepts through a reading of the theme of finitude. The problematic that remains might be seen as a tension between two faces of everyday life in Heidegger. The first face is the one toward which Heidegger expresses such mandarin antipathy. This is the everyday life of subjective claims and intersubjective structures of expectation: the experiential sphere within which our most important moral or ethical concepts play their roles. Heidegger could never see anything here other than more or less disguised iterations of the *Gestell*. The second face is the one Heidegger so beautifully illuminates in his later work: the experiential sphere within which we recollect or gesture our finitude and the place of otherness.

It is crucial not to allow this problem to slide into an easy resolution. For admirers of Heidegger's later work, there is a strong temptation to seize upon what he says about the appropriate attitude toward things and to simply *add* human beings to the list. Once over this hurdle, the way seems wide open to speculations about a Heideggerian ethics and politics. This is exactly the turn that Schürmann takes, although he provides no discussion of the textual support for his interpretation. Perhaps he finds the references to the plurality of human beings as "mortals"

---

51 For this charge, see Allan Megill, *Prophets of Extremity: Nietzsche, Heidegger, Foucault, Derrida* (Berkeley: University of California Press, 1985).
52 See texts cited in n. 45.

sufficient. But the references to mortals as one pole of *das Geviert* simply will not do.[53] The thought of mortals in relation to the other poles is not the same as the thought of mortals in relation to one another.

Another way of trying to get over the hurdle is to search for remarks on intersubjectivity scattered throughout Heidegger's corpus in the hope that they can be woven together with his second understanding of everyday life. There are, for example, the remarks on community I cited earlier; elsewhere Heidegger speaks of love and friendship.[54] But perhaps most tempting are the ones in *Being and Time* on "solicitude" or "care" [*Fürsorge*], especially the distinction made between genuine and "deficient" solicitude.[55] Such remarks are no doubt suggestive, but they remain no more than that. In the dense tropical jungle of Heideggerian discourse they are like small, stunted plants overshadowed by huge ones of a very different sort. One can speculate about how such plants might be nourished, but the Heideggerian antipathy toward the first face of everyday life always hangs over such attempts.[56] The problem here might be summed up by saying that it is difficult not to think that Heidegger would brook no dispute, no counterclaims, about how genuine solicitude should be realized in concrete situations of interaction. My conclusion is simply that no matter how we read Heidegger, and how we fold or place the parts in relation to one another, we cannot get over the difficulty that one attitude of face-to-faceness in everyday life is never adequately articulated with the other.

53 Schürmann, *Heidegger on Being and Acting,* pp. 60, 209–14, 240–4.
54 See the texts cited in n. 14.
55 *Being and Time,* pp. 158–9, 344–5.
56 Fred Dallmayr, for example, tries to project the vision of an ethics from these passages; see *Twilight of Subjectivity: Contributions to a Post-Individualist Theory of Politics* (Amherst: University of Massachusetts Press, 1981), pp. 64–71; and "Ontology of Freedom: Heidegger and Political Philosophy," *Political Theory* 12 (May 1984), pp. 214–15.

5

"FROM/AFTER THIS LAUGHTER AND THIS DANCE . . ."

My use of Heidegger to investigate the roots of postmodern thinking has suggested a twofold criticism. First, postmodernism tends to share the later Heidegger's difficulty in getting from an emphasis on responsibility to otherness and the world-disclosing dimension of language to an acceptable approach to ethics and politics. Further, postmodern thinking exhibits a persistent temptation to revel in a playful impertinence, thereby sometimes risking a loss of attention to what is most significant in its underlying orientation toward otherness. In this chapter I want to strengthen these criticisms by focusing more directly on Derrida (Section I), Lyotard (Section II), and, finally, Foucault and Richard Rorty (Section III). My aim here, however, is not the straightforward one of serial demolition. Just as important as the criticism is my attempt to construe the postmodern sensibility toward otherness in a way that echoes the insights I have drawn from the later Heidegger. There is much to learn here from these thinkers. And yet, by the end of the chapter, it is still the case that the topic of intersubjectivity, and thus ethics and politics, has not been adequately engaged. In the next chapter, it is suggested that this requires appropriating the insights of a certain strand of feminism.

I. Derrida's resituating of responsibility

Beginning roughly in the 1980s, there emerges a modification of tone and focus in at least some of Derrida's work. In these writings Derrida shows himself to be quite concerned about the charge that he and some of his adherents have too often succumbed to the temptation to let irresponsibility and impertinence dominate the activity of deconstruction.[1] He does not really engage in explicit self-criticism, but rather attempts to show more clearly the sense of "ethical–political responsibility" that is compatible with deconstruction.[2]

One prominent interpreter of Derrida has concluded that this shift of attention demonstrates an adherence to "the values of enlightened reason" and manifests "signs of convergence with the project of a critical theorist like Habermas."[3] Ultimately, there may be some truth in these assertions, but they tend to obscure more issues than they illuminate, in the sense of understanding the distinctive insights Derrida provides as well as the impasses he encounters. Such issues can be better explored using the concepts and distinctions I have deployed in the preceding chapters. In these terms, one can see Derrida's recent writings as a concerted attempt to explore the turn from the responsibility to otherness to the responsibility to act.

What is at issue can perhaps be brought to a head in the following passage from an essay Derrida wrote in the late 1960s. After learning the necessity of being not only impertinent before all the pretensions of metaphysical, metanarrative thinking, but also playfully impertinent in the Nietzschean sense, another question arises:

1 See especially Derrida, "Afterward: Toward an Ethic of Discussion," in *Limited Inc.* (Evanston, Ill.: Northwestern University Press, 1988), pp. 111–42. The subject of this afterward is his acrimonious debate with John Searle, one aspect of which was the impression left by Derrida that the sort of speech act theory Searle pursues is somehow implicated with "a police and a tribunal" (pp. 105, 131ff). This was elaborated upon by one of Derrida's adherents, who spoke of "the circuit that leads from John Searle's reactionary philosophical study to David Rockefeller's bank office, to the torture chambers of Santiago de Chile"; Michael Ryan, *Marxism and Deconstruction* (Baltimore: Johns Hopkins University Press, 1982), p. 46.
2 Derrida, *Limited Inc.*, pp. 116, 138.
3 Christopher Norris, *Derrida* (Cambridge, Mass.: Harvard University Press, 1987), pp. 157, 169.

From/after this laughter and this dance . . . what I will call Heideggerian *hope*, comes into question. I am not unaware how shocking this word might seem here. Nevertheless I am venturing it,
without excluding any of its implications. . . .[4]

What I wish to do in this section is think about the ethical–
political emphasis in Derrida's recent essays by asking how they
align themselves with the multiple valences of "Heideggerian
hope." For my purposes, two valences are crucial: the one emphasized in Chapter 3 (an utterly different, future politics), and the
other in Chapter 4 (an alternative experience of everyday life).

A

In Chapter 3, I showed how Heideggerian hope, construed in
terms of *das Kommende* and an other politics, constitutes a dead
end for rethinking the responsibility to act. Several of Derrida's
essays in the 1980s evoke notions such as "the future of another
law" and "a new kind of right and law" and attempt to explicate a
responsibility that can orient our collective action in such a new
direction.[5] Does this attempt to "resituate" the responsibility to
act render the idea of an other ethics and politics any more
plausible?[6]

As I understand Derrida, his notion of resituating responsibility refers to speaking the language of collective action, but in a
way that remains more attuned to the responsibility to otherness
than the dominant "juridical and egological" modes of practical
reason.[7] This resituated responsibility would be positioned in the
seam between the responsibility to act and the responsibility to
otherness. It would enable a discourse of ethical–political action

---

4 Derrida, "Différance," in *Margins of Philosophy,* trans. with additional notes by
  Alan Bass (Chicago: University of Chicago Press, 1982), p. 27; translation
  slightly altered.
5 Derrida, "Racism's Last Word," *Critical Inquiry* 12 (Autumn 1985), p. 298; and
  "The Conflict of Faculties: *A Mochlos,*" unpublished English translation, the
  essay appeared in French in *Philosophie* 2 (April 1984) p. 27. The dimension of
  responsibility in Derrida is thematized in Richard Bernstein, "Serious Play:
  The Ethical–Political Horizon of Jacques Derrida," *The Journal of Speculative
  Philosophy* I, No. 2 (1987), pp. 93–115.
6 Derrida, "The Principle of Reason: The University in the Eyes of Its Pupils,"
  Diacritics XIX (Fall 1983), p. 14.
7 Derrida, "The Conflict of Faculties," p. 26.

and yet retain "a constant, though oblique relation" to the problem of otherness.[8]

Derrida's efforts here are accompanied by figures familiar to the deconstructive elucidation of otherness – for example, the emphasis on attending to the "poetic" rather than the "informative value of language"; the focus on how reason demarcates itself from unreason; and on how we are constituted as subjects by our persistent desire to "render" things reasonable.[9] Other themes emerge, however, that point more directly toward the discourse of the responsibility to act, in particular those of *founding* and *friendship*.

One might explain Derrida's attention to foundational acts simply by recalling that the relevant papers were given on occasions commemorating specific institutional or political foundings.[10] Yet the focus on founding is also clearly theoretically determined. Founding documents and events often serve as anchors for ongoing discourses of legitimacy that surround institutions. Given the postmodern concern with metanarratives of legitimacy in the modern world, it is not surprising that Derrida is fascinated with exploring the status and self-understanding of such anchoring maneuvers. From this vantage point, the American Declaration of Independence becomes an exemplar of the dilemma of modern legitimacy. It continually tries to anchor itself in "constative" declarations about Nature or God, thereby hoping to provide an unimpeachable metanarrative ground for the actions of the colonists. This maneuver hides the radically "performative" character of the document: It creates a people and their rights. The "fabulous" quality of such foundational acts is crystalized in the paradox that the document is authorized by the signatures of the people's representatives, but the people and their representatives are themselves authorized by the performative utterances of the document.[11]

Derrida's deconstructive reading of the Declaration is intriguing and has the same potentially salutary effects of any such

8 Ibid., p. 14.
9 Ibid., pp. 30ff; and "The Principle of Reason," pp. 8–10, 14–15.
10 "The Principle of Reason" was given on the occasion of Derrida's occupying a chair named for Cornell University's first president; and "Declarations of Independence," *New Political Science* 15 (Summer 1986), pp. 7–15, was given at the University of Virginia on the occasion of the bicentennial of the American Declaration of Independence.
11 Derrida, "Declarations of Independence," pp. 9–11.

reading: It unsettles standard modes of legitimizing discourse, in this case explicitly political discourse.[12] But I want to press a particular issue here, and the best way to do it is to bring Heidegger back into the foreground. Heidegger's fascination with founding can serve as a foil against which to place Derrida's in order to get a better sense of how the latter might help resituate the responsibility to act. Now clearly, there is nothing in Derrida that remotely implies any affinity with Heidegger's attraction to the idea of a great leader/founder in the mold of Hitler. But just as clearly, there is a strong affinity between the two on the world-disclosive, performative character of some speech acts for political life. With this affinity, we are led directly back to the image of a radically other politics. Do Derrida's recent essays help us make more sense of this than Heidegger's appeal to *das Kommende*?

Derrida boldly refers us to "another founding site" where we can envision the "establishment of a new law, of a new epoch of right." Admittedly, Derrida has always been somewhat cautious when speaking of radical changes of terrain. One "cannot simply break with inherited tradition" and concepts.[13] However valid these cautions might be, they are never developed in a way that basically alters the momentum of Derrida's thinking. Ultimately their status is like that of signs on highways warning of the upcoming danger of falling rocks. One mentally files the warning and proceeds pretty much as before. Thus, in Derrida's discourse, what remains dominant is the image of the new foundation. One sees this well enough when he suggests that a resituating of responsibility will have to "negotiate a compromise with traditional right and law," but that the significance of this compromise lies primarily in furnishing "the support from which to leap toward another founding site." As a possible alternative to leaping, Derrida suggests the metaphor of a lever. The problem then is one of "determining the best lever or, the Greeks would say, *mochlos*."[14] In other words, we must focus on

12 For a thoughtful and sympathetic view of Derrida's essay, see B. Honig, "Declarations of Independence: Arendt and Derrida on the Problem of Founding a Republic," *The American Political Science Review* (85, No. 1, March 1991), pp. 97–113.

13 Derrida, "The Conflict of Faculties," pp. 77–8. Derrida's cautiousness is already evident in "The Ends of Man," *Margins of Philosophy*, p. 135. Norris makes much of this caution in his *Derrida* – too much, I argue later.

14 Derrida, "The Conflict of Faculties, p. 78.

the lever necessary to pry ethical–political discourse from its old foundation and shift it onto a new one.

It is difficult to see what is gained for a rethinking of the responsibility to act from the recourse to such mechanical metaphors. Although Derrida alludes to the Greeks, he really seems more in the company of eighteenth-century political thinkers. Perhaps mechanical metaphors can shed some light on things like constitutional or institutional structures; they seem particularly inappropriate, however, for understanding the kind of reorienting of political consciousness, commitment, and communication that Derrida appears to have in mind.

As noted in Chapter 2, critics have suggested that when it comes to the practical implications of deconstruction, Derrida persistently employs a withholding gesture. In his recent work on founding, with its appeal to another founding site, Derrida in effect both withholds and entices. He withholds elaboration of this other politics but entices us with its utter difference and the thrill of acting at the edge of the abyss.[15] Now he admits at one point that this attempt to resituate responsibility may be no more than a "negative wisdom" about ethics and politics.[16] But one might question whether much wisdom actually accompanies an image that so strongly reiterates what is implied in Heidegger's *das Kommende*.[17]

If the thematization of founding has relatively disappointing results, what about friendship? By focusing on the "politics of friendship," Derrida situates himself squarely within the terrain of intersubjectivity and the responsibility to act. Almost immediately he is negotiating his way through landmarks absent from his earlier work. Certainly the most startling is the idea that a "minimal community" or "a *sort* of friendship" is implied "in the sharing of a language (past or to come) and in the being-together that any allocution supposes."[18] Along with this minimal community in

15 Derrida is aware of the apocalyptic tone of some of his work, as well as the political dangers associated with it. See "Of an Apocalyptic Tone Recently Adopted in Philosophy," *Oxford Literary Review* VI, No. 2 (1984), pp. 17, 19, 29–34.

16 Derrida, "The Principle of Reason," p. 15.

17 See Thomas McCarthy's conclusion that Derrida's thinking is carried "inexorably . . . in the direction of the ineffable"; McCarthy, "The Politics of the Ineffable: Derrida's Deconstruction," *The Philosophical Forum* 1–2 (Fall–Winter 1989–90), pp. 146–68.

18 Derrida, "The Politics of Friendship," *The Journal of Philosophy* 11 (November 1988), pp. 632–44.

which one is always already embedded goes a "minimal responsibility." The pull of this responsibility results from the performative character of every utterance, every interpretation we make in ongoing interaction: "For one cannot interpret . . . without simultaneously proposing an institutional model, consolidating an existing model which makes possible this interpretation or producing a new model that accords with it." In every interpretation, "a concept of the institution is at work, a type of contract or model of an ideal seminar is constructed, a society is implied, repeated or displaced, transformed, threatened or destroyed."[19]

Deconstruction is now to be seen, at least partially, as a fulfilling of this responsibility implied in our ongoing linguistic interaction. One of its tasks, then, is tracing out the political implications of whatever models are implied in interpretations. This would seem to be a reemphasis of the thrust of poststructuralism in general that I noted in Chapter 2: "Give power no place to hide."[20] Now Derrida is aware of, and indeed affirms, the fact that this entails "taking a position." Yet even in this recent work, he does not provide any clue as to how such a position is to be normatively oriented.[21] The deficit here becomes all the more glaring when one notes some of the striking parallels with Habermas's notions of communicative rationality and ethics, focusing as they do on the imputations and responsibility implicit in ongoing interaction.[22] Here one might agree with Norris that Derrida is moving closer to Habermas, but the former seems strangely reluctant to tackle the host of questions that emerge from such a shift.

These problems with unpacking the normative implications of a minimal friendship only make one more perplexed as to why Derrida chooses friendship as "a privileged place for . . . reflection" on responsibility and politics. The answer comes in his analysis of the different senses of "response" and how they relate to friendship. The two senses Derrida finds most interesting are "responses" in the sense of "answer to" [*répondre a*] and "answer before" [*répondre devant*]. Here "we have two forms or dimen-

19 Derrida, "The Conflict of Faculties," pp. 52–6; "The Politics of Friendship," pp. 632–4.
20 Michael Shapiro, "Post-Structuralist Political Pedagogy," *News for Teachers of Political Science* (Winter 1985), p. 19.
21 Derrida, "The Conflict of Faculties," p. 56.
22 See Thomas McCarthy's response to Derrida in "On the Margins of Politics," *The Journal of Philosophy* 11 (November 1988), pp. 645–8.

sions of *respect* implied by any *responsibility.*" Both refer to an
"Other," but in the former case it is the "absolute singularity" of
the other that is stressed, whereas in the latter it is universality
that comes to the fore: "One answers before the law, a tribunal, a
jury authorized to represent the Other legitimately, in the form
of a moral, legal or political community." What fascinates Derrida most about friendship is how at its "very heart" it is constituted by this tension between, and "co-implication" of, particular
and universal responsibility. The great texts on friendship all
touch upon this phenomenon in various ways – for example, in
how they "*found and destabilize* at the same time" key binary distinctions such as private/public.[23]

The rationale for Derrida's privileging of friendship can now
be understood. By beginning one's reflections on politics and
responsibility in this way, one drops an anchor into the problematics of doing justice to the particular, concrete other in the hope
that this will withstand the strong currents of the universalizing,
abstractive discourse of modern political thought. Such an an-
chorage may indeed achieve this effect, but it remains unclear
how one is then to go on to do much real navigating at all in the
waters of political life. One must conclude that the focus on
friendship, just as on founding, at best yields reminders and
corrections to reflection on ethics and politics.

B

Derrida's recent turn toward the explication of a resituated responsibility to act thus appears to encounter substantial impasses. There are, however, some important and rather different insights to be gained from this work – although drawing
them out requires some reading against the grain. These insights
emerge if one reviews this work in terms of the themes I located
in the later Heidegger in Chapter 4: a different way of facing
everyday life, characterized by the play of *Nähe* and its associated
moods.

After this shift of attention, one notices something else in Derrida's discussion of friendship. As was indicated, he likes the way
the topic of friendship keeps distinctions such as that between
public and private in play. But he also elaborates upon a related

23 Derrida, "The Politics of Friendship," pp. 638–43.

play in a parenthetical remark. It is one he associates with Kant's analysis of friendship, where one of the "enigmas" of such a relationship comes from (in Derrida's words) the "distance or . . . respectful separation which distinguishes it, as a feeling, from love." In friendship, there must be an "unstable equilibrium of the two feelings that are opposed in the mode of 'attraction' that tends toward fusion (love) and 'repulsion' that holds at a distance (respect)."[24] When this becomes the center of reflection on friendship, one is not led to interrogate that relationship primarily as a possible structure of obligations that can provide a direct normative orientation for political action; rather, its significance now is as a mode of experience typified by a complex of feelings. One begins to suspect here that what is of value in Derrida's reflections is the sketching of a postmodern sensibility toward otherness, whose roots lie at least partially in Heidegger's thoughts about experiencing everyday life.

If one puts this sensibility at the center of attention, one can reengage Derrida's fascination with founding and open up some new questions. In the earlier discussion I drew attention to the fabulous, world-disclosive dimension of founding. But Derrida also points out that every opening of new ground [*Grund*] springs forth from the "*abyss*" [*Abgrund*] into the light.[25] Constant attention to this quality of founding must be maintained; otherwise, institutions will appear to be more securely anchored in certainties than they really are. In the essay that makes reference to the establishment of Cornell University, Derrida applauds the wisdom of the founders' having sited the institution near a deep gorge.

What is at issue here, however, is not just a concern with otherness expressed by undermining the false self-confidence of foundations; it also has to do with the moods Derrida sees as appropriate counterparts to reflection upon such human events. These moods are the ones traditionally associated with the experience of the sublime (as distinct from the beautiful). A sense of the sublime is elicited when one is faced with the abyss, the gigantic, the monstrous. Moods typically associated with such experiences are awe, anxiety, and an exalted desperation.[26] Although Derrida discusses the sublime specifically in relation to founding, there is a

24 Ibid., p. 640, n. 7.
25 Derrida, "The Principle of Reason," p. 6.
26 Ibid.

real sense in which the sublime and its moods are deeply involved with the entire project of deconstruction. Referring to one of his early texts, Derrida asserts that what he intends is "a violent production of meaning" that, although working "through tradition, emerges at a given moment as a *monster*, a monstrous mutation without tradition or normative precedent."[27]

This connection of deconstruction with the sublime, and especially the peculiarly ambivalent moods with which it is associated, brings out another way in which Derrida's thinking echoes key themes in Heidegger's later work. Nevertheless, there is a distinct difference in tone. Earlier I said that Heidegger's other thinking aims at a reorienting of experience so as to allow the "ubiquity of the finite" quietly into everyday life. The notion of the sublime, as Derrida uses it, has a quality that draws us in a different direction: an emphasis on the monstrous, the shocking. Why is there this emphasis, and what effect does it have on a mode of thought attuned in the first instance to elucidating the responsibility to otherness? In one sense, Derrida is hardly taking a surprising position; the association of the sublime with the monstrous is quite familiar, going back originally to the seminal reflections of Edmund Burke.[28] But Derrida is hardly one to embrace traditional conceptions uncritically. Hence, it probably makes sense to see his attraction to monstrosity as reflecting deconstruction's avowed aims of impertinently intervening in everyday life in ways that jolt normal sensibility. And the more monstrous the intervention, the more effective the jolt.

Here one sees Derrida giving in to that typical temptation of postmodernism alluded to in Chapter 4: allowing the impulse of intervention to overshadow other impulses in postmodern reflection. It is Lyotard rather than Derrida who makes more headway in resisting this temptation, and he thus opens up a more promising path for thinking about how the sublime and a postmodern sensibility should be related.

---

27 "Deconstruction and the Other," in Richard Kearney, ed., *Dialogues with Contemporary Continental Thinkers* (Manchester: Manchester University Press, 1984), p. 123.

28 Edmund Burke, "A Philosophical Inquiry into the Origin of Our Ideas of the Sublime and Beautiful," in *The Works of the Right Honorable Edmund Burke* (Boston: Little, Brown, 1881), pp. 110–11, 130–41. See Jean-François Lyotard, "The Sublime and the Avant-Garde," in Andrew Benjamin, ed., *The Lyotard Reader* (Oxford: Basil Blackwell, 1989). See n. 29.

II. Toward a sublime of everyday life

Lyotard has been consistently fascinated with developing a way of thinking about the sublime as the core of a postmodern sensibility that can resist the homogenizing, normalizing forces of societal rationalization.[29] He builds upon the classical analyses of the sublime in Burke and Kant, but he breaks with them in ways that directly engage the themes I have been following.

Lyotard attaches his explanation of the sublime to concerns that dominate Heidegger's later work. What is at issue is a mode of experience, the point of which is "to become open to the 'It happens that' rather than to the 'What happens'."[30] The asking of "What happens" expresses a proto-rationalizing, technologizing attitude. Attention to the "It happens," on the other hand, is what Heidegger grappled with under the notion of *Ereignis*, the presencing–absencing of being. For Lyotard, when we feel the sublime, it opens us to a "bearing . . . witness" to this presencing/absencing.[31]

The central structural feature of the sublime is the experience of an ambivalent or "contradictory feeling."[32] As was mentioned earlier, such a feeling emerges through a peculiar juxtaposing of pleasurable with painful or distressing sensations. It is the way that Lyotard rethinks this feeling and what calls it forth that is of present interest. Following Kant, Lyotard sees the painfulness of the sublime arising from being confronted with what is terrifying, huge, or monstrous. The confrontation is distressing because the mind experiences its own limitations. And yet there is also a peculiar pleasure. Although our imagination cannot comprehend the object confronted, that object lets the mind discover "that it can conceive of something like the infinite." Thus the "pleasure comes from the use of reason," but in a way that involves the disengagement "of all grasping intelligence and of its

29 Lyotard, "The Sublime and the Avant-Garde," *The Lyotard Reader*, pp. 209–11; and *The Differend: Phrases in Dispute*, trans. by Georges Van Den Abbeele (Minneapolis: University of Minnesota Press, 1988), pp. xv, 181.
30 Lyotard, *Peregrinations: Law, Form, Event* (New York: Columbia University Press, 1988), pp. 18, 28.
31 Lyotard, "The Sublime and the Avant-Garde," *Lyotard Reader*, pp. 197–9. See Heidegger's discussion of "Es gibt" in "Time and Being," in *On Time and Being*, trans. by Joan Stambaugh (New York: Harper and Row, 1972), pp. 5ff; see esp. n. 1 on p. 5.
32 Lyotard, "The Sublime and the Avant-Garde," *Lyotard Reader*, p. 198.

power."[33] The Idea of infinity, like all Kantian Ideas, is raised above the phenomenal world of cause and effect and all human motivations. We can only contemplate this element of the noumenal world.

Lyotard modifies this Kantian analysis with the intention of envisioning a sensibility for what I would like to call the "sublime of everyday life." His ideas here are quite instructive, and yet they ultimately offer an unsatisfactory direction for this rethinking of the sublime in the context of a postmodern sensibility.

In order to understand what Lyotard is up to, it is necessary to elucidate briefly the theory of language he offers in *The Differend*.[34] The essential components of language are, according to Lyotard, "phrases"; "phrase regimens: reasoning, knowing, describing, recounting, questioning, showing, ordering, etc."; and "genres of discourses." The last of these "supply rules for linking together heterogeneous phrases," each arising from some phrase regimen. These rules are ones that are proper for attaining certain goals: "to know, to teach, to be just, to seduce, to justify, to evaluate, to rouse emotion, to oversee."[35]

Lyotard postulates several essential characteristics of this constellation of linguistic phenomena. The appearance of a phrase is the irreducible "It happens." It is the most basic particle of heterogeneity, particularity; each phrase discloses or "presents at least one universe."[36] But phrases are always "linked onto" in some way by genres of discourse (in the sense that a given phrase might be enlisted into a discourse of seduction, or of justification, or of command, and so on). And genres of discourse are themselves radically heterogeneous, "since the success proper to one genre is not the one proper to others." What this means is a perpetual "conflict between genres of discourse": Every linkage onto a phrase constitutes "a kind of 'victory' of one of them over the other. These others remain neglected, forgotten, or repressed possibilities."[37] The final essential characteristic of language is the "differend," by which Lyotard means the "wrong" that necessarily occurs to the "losing" genre of discourse "whose possible phrases remain unactualized." The "wrong" is a neces-

---

33 Ibid., pp. 199, 203–4; and *Peregrinations*, p. 40.
34 Lyotard, *The Differend*.
35 Ibid., p. xii.
36 Ibid., pp. xii, 70.
37 Ibid., pp. 136–7.

sary one because there can be no "rule of judgment" common to genres of discourse that can resolve the conflicts impartially.[38]

There should be no anthropocentric misunderstanding of this picture of language. The conflict between genres of discourse does not rest upon human will or intention: "Genres of discourse are strategies – of no one." And, more generally, language should not be thought of as something man uses "for his own ends." In fact "language is not a language, but phrases" that simply "happen." The image Lyotard presents us with is thus ultimately one without human subjects; there is only the occurrence of phrases and the conflicts between genres of discourse, leaving victors who have wronged the vanquished.[39]

In terms of the characterization that I have given of postmodern thinkers as a whole, one can easily see what concerns inform Lyotard's picture of language. The sense of responsibility to otherness and the privileging of the world-disclosive capacity of language come together in Lyotard's notions of the "It happens" of each phrase; in the differend or wrong to the other that necessarily accompanies its linkage to further phrases; and, finally, in his injunction that we must "bear witness to the differend." It is in the heterogeneity of the "It happens" and the differend, Lyotard maintains, that one finds "the only insurmountable obstacle" to the increasing rationalization of social life, understood now as the "hegemony of the economic genre."[40]

What is of specific interest in the immediate context is how this way of understanding language and otherness is linked to Lyotard's notion of the sublime. What he apparently is attempting to do is to draw the feeling of the sublime out of any necessary relation to monstrousness.[41] The "It happens" is now associated not with the monstrous and shocking, but with the mundane appearance of every phrase. By conceptualizing language as he does, Lyotard wants to show that the experience of the sublime can and should be awakened at the most basic level of everyday life.

But what surrogate now steps in for monstrosity as the immediate impetus for distress and pleasure in the feeling of the sublime? The distress emerges from the "threat" and "anxiety" that

38 Ibid., pp. xi–xii.
39 Ibid., pp. xiii, 137–8, 141.
40 Ibid., pp. xii, 181.
41 Lyotard, *Peregrinations*, p. 41.

occur at the "gap" between one phrase and its linkage to another, and at the "abyss that separates heterogeneous genres of discourse." Here, in everyday life, one comes *face to face* with nothingness" – with the experience that the event of the phrase and its linkage to others is "not necessary and is scarcely foreseeable."[42] The pleasure of this everyday sublime emerges from the Idea (in the Kantian sense) of "a possible passage" over the abyss of heterogeneity. This Idea inspires us, but the reality of a heterogeneity that goes (as Richard Rorty likes to say) "all the way down" cannot really be tamed by the human mind, except through self-deception. At a collective level, this is just what modernity is guilty of when it forges passages over difference with the aid of foundational metanarratives.[43] If this is illegitimate, however, what does the Idea of "a possible passage" mean? Apparently it is not a unidirectional movement that methodically brings instances of otherness into an imperium. Rather it is "a kind of agitation in place, one within the impasse of incommensurability, and above the abyss." There is an attraction to the possibility of a passage and a repulsion from the hubris of forging it.[44]

If one surveys the foregoing vista of language and the sublime, one is struck by the interesting attempt to elaborate a postmodern sensibility in terms of a sublime of everyday life but also by the implausibility of the theory of language in terms of which that elaboration proceeds. It is relatively easy to show that phrases, phrase regimens, and genres of discourse are in fact not so immaculately heterogeneous and autonomous, but rather inextricably interwoven with one another. And it is difficult to see much sense in Lyotard's hyper-juridification of linguistic phenomena. Why are "wrongs" sewn into every bit of language, especially since Lyotard is at such pains to paint a picture of language "happening" above the heads, as it were, of human beings?[45] These and other problems lead one quickly to the conclusion that the main attraction of this picture is its claimed

42 Ibid., pp. 17–18, 32; *Differend*, pp. 143, 179; "The Sublime and the Avant-Garde," *Lyotard Reader*, p. 199, my emphasis.
43 *Differend*, pp. 179–80.
44 Ibid., p. 167. Lyotard also sometimes uses "idioms" instead of "passages" in this context: "One's responsibility before thought consist[s] of detecting differends and . . . finding the (impossible) idiom for phrasing them. This is what a philosopher does" (p. 142).
45 See the sympathetic but devastating criticism of Lyotard in Wolfgang Welsch, *Unsere postmoderne Moderne* (Weinheim: VCH, 1987), pp. 247–58.

practical usefulness for combatting the homogenizing expansion of the economic genre of discourse.

But there is another problem besides the one related to language. It is rather surprising to find Lyotard fleshing out the notion of a postmodern sensibility in a way so heavily dependent on Kant's noumenal world of Ideas. It is the contemplation of this world that ultimately is the source of pleasure in the sublime. As with the picture of language, the practical attraction of invoking the world of Ideas is quite clear: The mind is humbled in relation to it. However, this invocation also entails a host of familiar conceptual problems. Given the intellectual commitments of postmodernism, it is difficult to see how Lyotard would be able to sustain such a sharp distinction between the noumenal and phenomenal worlds.

One problem in particular is worth mentioning. Lyotard is right that the experience of the sublime humbles the mind in the sense of exhibiting limits to its ability to grasp and comprehend. But in another sense, the experience of the sublime in Kant raises us, as rational beings, out of nature: "we . . . become conscious of our superiority to nature within us, and thereby also to nature outside us (as far as it influences us)."[46] Is such an elevation of human being not deeply implicated in that whole history of privileging willful subjectivity, against which postmodernism has directed so much criticism? At the very least, Lyotard must realize that his dependence on Kant raises as many problems as it is intended to solve.

If one were to drop this reliance on Kant and the implausible view of language, what would be left of Lyotard's sketch of postmodern sensibility? The answer, I think, is his effort to elucidate an experience of the sublime on the everyday level, that is, in a way that does not have to be incited by the monstrous, shocking event. Here one can begin to weave together Lyotard's aim with the ideas I drew out of Heidegger.

In an essay written a number of years before *The Differend*, Lyotard seems to favor Burke over Kant on the subject of the sublime. For Burke, the pain of the sublime is associated with the terror of privation, especially the threat of impending death. The pleasure of the sublime occurs, in Lyotard's words, when

46 Kant, *Critique of Judgment*, trans. by Werner Pluhar (Indianapolis, Ind.: Hackett, 1987), p. 123.

such a "terror-causing threat [is] suspended, kept at bay, held back." Art that can distance the menace elicits "a pleasure of relief, of delight. Thanks to art, the soul is returned to the agitated zone between life and death, and this agitation is its health and life."[47] Given this admiration of Burke, it is interesting to speculate about what would emerge if one deflated Burke's terror-inducing confrontation with finitude and thought of an experience of the sublime constituted in relation to allowing finitude quietly into everyday life.

A postmodern sensibility would then both measure the world in a distinct way and constitute the contradictory feelings of the sublime in a distinct way. The sense of finitude would come alive in the spacing between the self and otherness. The delight with the appearance of the other brings with it the urge to draw it closer. But that urge must realize its limits, beyond which the drawing nearer becomes a gesture of grasping. And that realization will be palpable only when we are sensitive to the appearance of the particular other as testimony of finitude. Then delight will be paired with a sense of grief or mourning at the fragility and momentary quality of the appearance of the other. Something like this, it seems to me, is not so far from what is at the heart of Lyotard's intention of bearing witness to the differend at the level of everyday life.

III. A bearable lightness of care

In the foregoing, I have read Derrida and Lyotard in a way that amplifies one voice in which they try to address otherness and tones down the voice of impertinence, the voice that shocks. In this way, one hears things not so different from Heidegger. But this further explanation of the responsibility to otherness still has not really made much headway on the problems of intersubjectivity, ethics, and politics. Lyotard admits that bearing witness in his sense does not "make a political 'program,' " but he wants to contend that it is nevertheless in some sense political.[48] That sense, however, is only evoked, never made tangible. (I will return to this question in Chapter 7.)

A provocative way of beginning to move from a postmodern

47 Lyotard, "The Sublime and the Avant-Garde," *Lyotard Reader*, pp. 204–5.
48 Lyotard, *Differend*, pp. xiii, 140–2, 181.

sensibility toward the constellation of questions involved with the responsibility to act is hinted at in the work of Foucault and Rorty. One could try to uncover such an opening in several places in Foucault's later work – for example, in the last two volumes of *The History of Sexuality* or perhaps in his brief remarks on dialogue.[49] I want to locate the opening in a different spot, however, whose significance perhaps becomes fully evident only when one places some of Rorty's insights next to it.

What does Foucault mean when he muses: "I dream of a new age of curiosity"? He explains:

> Curiosity . . . I like the word. . . . It evokes "care"; it evokes the care one takes of what exists and what might exist; a sharpened sense of reality, but one that is never immobilized before it; a readiness to find what surrounds us strange and odd; a certain determination to throw off familiar ways of thought and to look at the same things in a different way.[50]

Foucault admits that traditionally, in Christianity for example, curiosity has hardly been thought to be a virtue. And yet he clearly sees it as such; moreover, he associates it specifically with care, although he surrounds the word with quotation marks. Why this association, and why the quotation marks?

The second question is probably easier to answer. Not surprisingly, Foucault wants to maintain a distance from some of the connotations of care. Care always harbors the danger that the

---

49 See Foucault, *History of Sexuality*, Vol. 2: *The Use of Pleasure*, trans. by Robert Hurley (New York: Pantheon, 1985); *History of Sexuality*, Vol. 3: *The Care of the Self*, trans. by Robert Hurley (New York: Pantheon, 1986); and "On the Genealogy of Ethics: An Overview of Work in Progress" and "Polemics, Politics, and Problematizations: An Interview with Michel Foucault," in Paul Rabinow, ed., *The Foucault Reader* (New York: Pantheon, 1984), pp. 381–90. My concerns about the fruitfulness of Foucault's remarks on dialogue parallel those expressed earlier in this chapter in regard to Derrida. As for the notions of "care of the self" and an "aesthetics of existence," I do not mean to imply that they are of no interest at all to ethics; rather, I simply see no evidence that they produce any substantial insights into the broad range of ethical–political issues upon which I am focusing in the present context. For similar skepticism in this regard, see Thomas McCarthy, "The Critique of Impure Reason: Foucault and the Frankfurt School," *Political Theory* 18 (August 1990), 437–69.

50 Foucault, "The Masked Philosopher," in Lawrence D. Kritzman, ed., *Politics, Philosophy, Culture: Interviews and Other Writings 1977–1984*, trans. by Alan Sheridan and others (New York and London: Routledge, Chapman and Hall, 1988), p. 328. I thank Bill Connolly for drawing my attention to this theme.

caregiver will overshelter the other, smother or envelop him or her in a blanket of paternalistic (or maternalistic) control. This is the same sort of concern I expressed about Heidegger's *Fürsorge* in *Being and Time*, and it parallels some of Derrida's worries about Heidegger.[51]

The association of curiosity with care allies this wariness of overbearing modes of care with a positive emphasis on a fine-grained attention to the concrete details of the lives of others. In general, one might say that the pairing of curiosity and care is aimed at fostering a certain lightness of care. One can flesh this out a bit more by turning to Rorty's thinking about the central role of curiosity in the possible retuning of our sensitivity toward one another. Rorty's elevation of curiosity to the level of a primary virtue is most easily understood by beginning with the vice with which it is contrasted. Cruelty is the greatest vice in Rorty's moral world. Typically, it is easy to recognize, but it has one everyday form that is relatively inconspicuous: "incuriosity." This mundane cruelty is manifested in a simple lack of concern or attention to the ways in which concrete others suffer in everyday life. With the vice so defined, the corresponding virtue of curiosity then takes the form of a concerned attitude to the details of the lives of others.[52]

The sort of curiosity Rorty has in mind emerges from an aesthetic sensibility rather than a rigorous philosophical attitude.[53] But not just any aesthetic sensibility will do. In this regard, Rorty reminds us that a refined, aesthetic sensibility can easily be combined with extraordinary incuriosity. Vladimir Nabokov was a master at portraying characters of this sort: the "monster of incuriosity," such as Humbert Humbert in *Lolita*.[54] The particular type of aesthetic sensibility Rorty wants to endorse is that of the novelist, with her "taste for narrative, detail, diversity, and accident."[55] Charles Dickens is the positive arche-

51 Derrida, as I noted in Chapter 4, is worried about the images of sheltering, preserving, homeland, and so on.
52 Richard Rorty, *Contingency, Irony and Solidarity* (Cambridge: Cambridge University Press, 1989), pp. 158–68; and "Philosophers, Novelists and Inter-Cultural Comparisons: Heidegger, Kundera, and Dickens," paper presented to the Sixth East-West Philosopher's Conference, Honolulu, July 31–August 11, 1989, p. 19.
53 Rorty, "Philosophers, Novelists and Intercultural Comparisons," p. 14.
54 Rorty, *Contingency, Irony and Solidarity*, p. 161.
55 Rorty, "Philosophers, Novelists, and Intercultural Comparisons," p. 14.

type here. He was able to merge an aesthetic appreciation of the inexhaustible plurality of humanity with a persistent concern for the suffering and injustice he saw in the streets around him. Moreover, this attitude did not succumb to the temptation of thinking that *really* caring required some sort of total transformation of consciousness and society, as so many socialists of Dickens's time believed. This, to Rorty's mind, is the most effective way to meet the responsibility to otherness.

The limits of Rorty's line of thinking can be seen if one considers the way Rorty links it to the problems of politics. His admiration for Dickens's moderation in regard to the need for transforming consciousness and society is aimed primarily not at nineteenth-century socialists but at contemporary revolutionaries of all kinds, as well as those postmoderns who evoke images of a radically "other" politics as the only salvation from the incessant spread of societal rationalization, normalization, the *Gestell*, and so on. For Rorty, social ills in a *liberal* society require no transformation to be alleviated; rather, Dickens teaches us that suffering or injustice "has merely to be noticed to be remedied."[56]

Rorty admits that this assumption is often empirically untrue, but he seems, by and large, to think that in contemporary Western societies it is true.[57] What we need to do to foster a greater sense of curiosity today is simply to read more novels and see more docudramas on television.[58] Perhaps in something close to the best of all possible social worlds this would be true. The problem is that Rorty, in his eagerness to distance himself from all those who launch strong critiques of modern social life, comes close to implying that we now live in something like the best of all possible social worlds. He reduces our possible practical stances toward contemporary society to two: Either persist in seeking some misbegotten image of a totally "other" politics or seat yourself on the sofa and tune in to a docudrama.

Rorty is astonishingly unconcerned with certain qualities of contemporary society. What does he make of the fact that in the United States the sorts of novels he prefers are disappearing from the shelves of the huge chain bookstores to make way for Harlequin Romances; or that the sort of docudrama he envisions is the extreme exception, with the rule being ones that are glitzy,

56 Ibid., pp. 27–9.
57 Ibid., p. 29.
58 Rorty, *Contingency, Irony and Solidarity*, p. xvi.

sensationalist, and full of stereotypes offensive to women, for example? Rorty fails to take seriously such phenomena associated with societal rationalization and informationalization because he seems to feel that if you dwell upon them, you are thereby necessarily tainted with visions of total transformation. But this is really just a confusion of the phenomena of the postmodern problematic with one sort of response to it. Moreover, this confusion threatens to undermine Rorty's own useful insights about curiosity. By picturing this virtue as something adequately fostered by current patterns of watching television, he runs the risk of transforming a lightness of care into a "liteness."

If one takes the postmodern problematic more seriously, one will want to reflect a bit further than Rorty on curiosity/care. One will find it necessary for this kind of care to be rooted in an orientation to finitude that resists the desperate drives to infinities of knowledge and control that inhere within processes of societal rationalization and informationalization. I would suggest that the kind of orientation toward finitude I have explored so far will fill this need. Its mood (contradictory feelings) and measure (the space of attraction and repulsion) will sustain a lightness of care: They will resist the urge to dominate the other, as well as the temptation to liteness, to a postmodern chinoiserie.

If some progress has been made in this chapter in further elucidating a postmodern way of responding to the sense of responsibility to otherness, not much has yet been achieved in exploring the linkage between this sensibility and the way the topics of intersubjectivity, ethics, and politics emerge within reflection responding to the responsibility to act. The notion of a lightness of care now provides a certain initial bearing.

6

DIFFERENCE FEMINISM AND RESPONSIBILITY TO OTHERNESS

I have elucidated the sense of responsibility to otherness that emerges in Heidegger and followed it through the work of some contemporary postmodern thinkers. In the latter I suggested that, if one looks beyond the attitude of impertinence, one finds the trail of a sensibility whose qualities and focus on everyday life strongly echo Heidegger's concerns. This sensibility was then interpreted as possibly expressing itself in an attitude of care for the other. And yet the contours and implications of this attitude are barely suggested. These sorts of issues have been explored extensively, however, within feminist discussions of the last few years.

The wing of feminism that has focused most closely on the idea of care and its ethical–political implications is sometimes referred to as "difference feminism." This wing has explored qualities of everyday experience that (1) have been neglected or subordinated in prevailing conceptions of ethics and politics and that (2) are more prevalent in the lives of women. Carol Gilligan is undoubtedly the best-known representative of this approach.[1]

---

1 Carol Gilligan, *In a Different Voice* (Cambridge, Mass.: Harvard University Press, 1982). See Sara Ruddick, "Maternal Thinking," *Feminist Studies* 6, no. 3 (Summer 1980), pp. 342–67; Jean Bethke Elshtain, "Antigone's Daughters," *Democracy* 2 (April 1982), pp. 46–59; and Eva Feder Kittay and Diana T. Meyers, eds., *Women and Moral Theory* (Totowa, N.J.: Roman and Littlefield, 1987).

She has proposed a distinction between an ethic of "responsibility and care" and an "ethic of justice." The latter is expressed in the work of social contractarians, Kantians, and Habermas (to a degree), and it constructs its ethical–political world around the concepts of separate and autonomous subjects who balance claims and rights against one another according to universal principles. The idea of an ethics of responsibility and care, on the other hand, emerges from the experience of connectedness, compassion, and sensitivity to context.[2]

Affinities between feminism in general and postmodernism have often been noted, especially in regard to their common questioning of the dominant metanarratives of modern Western life.[3] This is certainly true, but my present interest is focused more specifically on the notion of care. I intend to show that the two ways of approaching this notion can mutually inform one another. When the difference feminist account is understood in relation to the two senses of responsibility, it becomes easier to see why the orientation toward care is not adequately described either as a separate "women's morality" or as a self-sufficient ethical orientation for contemporary life (Section I). Alternatively, when the idea of a postmodern sensibility is joined with feminist discussions of care, one gets better insights into the problem of intersubjectivity, ethics, and politics (Section II). A major criticism that has to be allayed here is the persistent worry that an orientation to care is ethically appropriate only for intimate spheres like the family and the relationship between friends.

I. The significance of care in feminism

It is often suggested that difference feminism, with its orientation to care and associated values, boils down to a "women's morality"

2 Gilligan, *In a Different Voice*, pp. 19, 30, 73 passim; and "Do the Social Sciences Have an Adequate Theory of Moral Development?" in Norma Haan et al., eds., *Social Science as Moral Inquiry* (New York: Columbia University Press, 1983), pp. 34–40.
3 See Nancy Fraser and Linda J. Nicholson, "Social Criticism without Philosophy: An Encounter between Feminism and Postmodernism," and the literature cited in their n. 1, in Linda J. Nicholson, ed., *Feminism/Postmodernism* (New York: Routledge, 1990), p. 35. See also Alice Jardine, *Gynesis: Configurations of Women and Modernity* (Ithaca, N.Y.: Cornell University Press, 1985); and Kathy Ferguson, *The Feminist Case against Bureaucracy* (Philadelphia: Temple University Press, 1984).

and thereby redirects feminism as a whole backward toward the idea of a special – and subordinate – place for women in social life.[4] Part of the problem here may reflect the fact that difference feminism is sometimes seen as proposing an alternative morality that is rooted in female biology.[5] But Gilligan does not speak this way. She and others (the sophisticated difference feminists) repeatedly emphasize that they do not espouse such a connection.[6] The claim is simply that, given prevailing socialization patterns and the traditional position of women in the family, certain values are typically woven more deeply into the fabric of women's everyday lives than of men's. The inappropriateness of accusing such thinkers of purveying a purely women's morality can be seen by suggesting a parallel accusation of Marx. Would it make sense to charge Marx with having said that no one but an industrial worker could learn the value of solidarity? Clearly, it would not. What he, and the socialist tradition in general, did was, first, to locate the force of this value in the lives of a particular segment of capitalist society; second, to demonstrate how the dominant modes of social life eviscerate commitment to such a value; and, third, project a vision of a future society in which solidarity is an integral component. I am suggesting that one should think about the claims of difference feminism in a roughly parallel fashion.

If this makes sense, the interesting questions in regard to difference feminism have to do with the coherence and general significance of the values it has been emphasizing, as well as the possibility of envisioning a public life that is more strongly informed by these values.[7] I want to approach these topics by placing them within the framework of the two senses of responsibility. This requires first showing how the value of care is explicated by feminists in ways that have strong affinities with Heidegger and the postmoderns.

4 See, for example, the critiques of Gilligan in the symposium "On *In a Different Voice:* An Interdisciplinary Forum," in *Signs* 11, no. 2 (Winter 1986), pp. 304–33.

5 See, for example, Ferguson, *The Feminist Case against Bureaucracy*, p. 28.

6 Although this reading may reflect legitimate political concerns about the *reception* of difference feminism in the dominant culture, that does not alter the fact that it is a misreading, as a careful look at the "Introduction" to *In a Different Voice* should make clear. See also Gilligan's response in the issue of *Signs* cited in footnote 4, as well as Ruddick, "Maternal Thinking," p. 346.

7 Another interesting question concerns the place of these values in the lives of other subordinated groups in modern society. See Joan Tronto, "Beyond Gender Difference to a Theory of Care," *Signs* 12, no. 4 (1987), pp. 644–63.

In the later work of Heidegger, the relationship of human being and being has a peculiarly engaged attitude that, following Heidegger, I have called face-to-faceness. I contrasted this in Chapter 4 with the systematically disengaged attitude often evident in postmodern thinking. Feminists have also tended to be somewhat suspicious of this disengagement and its implications for ethics and politics, while at the same time searching for models of face-to-faceness that relativize the validity of the dominant ones.[8] This orientation of feminism in general, and of difference feminism in particular, has given it a unique position in contemporary thought. No other mode of thought so successfully and continually alerts us to the shift of gravitational force that occurs at the seam of the responsibility to act and to otherness. And no other mode of thought probes so interestingly the question of how to act and yet remain attentive to otherness. With these themes in mind, I want to elucidate the qualities of experience that difference feminism emphasizes and that emerge from the analysis of situations and relationships where human needs, emotions, and demands confront one another.

In *In a Different Voice*, Gilligan contrasts the reactions of boys and girls to hypothetical moral dilemmas. But, unlike her mentor, Lawrence Kohlberg, she understands this contrast in a way that does not present the girls' reaction as simply a deficient form of the boys'. For present purposes, what is most interesting is how the boys excel in the speed and certainty with which they resolve the dilemmas. A moral dilemma is construed as "a math problem with humans." The important thing is to grasp hold of the problem and reduce it to terms that allow its clear-cut resolution, thereby freeing us to act in a situation we have brought under cognitive control.[9] The point of such thinking is, of course, to minimize harm to the moral values we rank most highly. Girls, on the other hand, often hesitate before a given resolution. Gilligan rejects the dominant view that hesitancy of this sort implies merely confusion over moral judgment. On the contrary, what is at issue is a deeper sense of the harmfulness of action, a sensitivity

8 See, for example, Ferguson, *The Feminist Case against Bureaucracy*, and Nancy Hartsock, "Epistemology and Politics: Developing Alternatives to Western Political Thought," paper delivered at the meeting of the International Political Science Association, Washington, D.C., August 1988.
9 Gilligan, *In a Different Voice*, p. 26. See also Ruddick, "Maternal Thinking," p. 350.

to the harm done to concrete others and relationships in the abstractive "mathmaticizing" of human moral confrontations.[10]

Now this kind of sensitivity to the "violence" of many of our standard modern modes of thinking is something shared by feminism, Heidegger, and contemporary postmodernism.[11] I have shown how the last two have struggled to become clearer about the contours of the orientation in terms of which this deepened perception of violence is located. The difference feminists' efforts to elucidate such an orientation, however, have been more persistent and have focused directly on intersubjectivity.[12] Their work has intensively investigated the posture of attentive care for concrete, specific others and the relationships in which we stand with them. Now there are many senses of "care," ranging from exercising care in opening a door for someone to the total care one must show to a newborn child or a terminally ill elder.[13] For present concerns, it is human interaction that falls somewhere in the middle of this range that is most relevant. The most important question here is, what precisely are the qualities associated with an attitude of care in such situations? I want to open up this question by drawing attention to significant affinities between, on the one hand, Heidegger's other thinking and a postmodern sensibility and, on the other hand, the feminist understanding of care. These affinities focus on the distinctive mood and measure I have identified in the former.

To exercise attentive care requires, of course, that one draw the other into one's own interpretive frame; but this "drawing in" has features that distinguish it from the straightforward procedures of abstraction and the stating and ranking of different claims. Care requires a much stronger "injunction to listen" to the other, a willingness to hold open an intersubjective space in which difference can unfold in its particularity.[14] This willingness entails a hesitancy to "place" the other quickly and firmly

10 Gilligan, "Do the Social Sciences . . . ," pp. 30–1; and *In a Different Voice*, p. 66.
11 See Jacques Derrida, "Violence and Metaphysics: An Essay on the Thought of Emmanuel Levinas," in *Writing and Difference*, trans. and introduced by Alan Bass (Chicago: University of Chicago Press, 1978), pp. 79–153.
12 This does not mean that feminists have not also been concerned with nonhuman nature, something that is prevalent in "eco-feminism."
13 For an elucidation of modes of caring, see Berenice Fisher and Joan Tronto, "Toward a Feminist Theory of Caring," in Emily Abel and Margaret Nelson, eds., *Circles of Caring* (Albany, N.Y.: State University of New York Press, 1989), pp. 35–62.
14 Gilligan, "Do the Social Sciences . . . ," p. 23; *In a Different Voice*, pp. 28–30.

within habitual interpretive molds. "If difference is to emerge there must first be silence, a willing suspension of habitual speech."[15]

In a relationship of care, excessive control of the other is recognized as a distinct liability. In discussing the orientation implied in "maternal thinking," Ruddick argues that it is animated by a "metaphysical" attitude of "holding" over that of grasping or acquiring. "Holding" here means recognition of the fragility of the concrete other and attention to preserving and repairing relationships.[16]

The affinity of such an attitude of care with Heidegger's "other thinking" should be evident, especially in regard to its contrast with attitudes Heidegger subsumed under the concept of the *Gestell*. But the affinity goes further. It will be remembered that *Nähe* was Heidegger's description of how to posture our thinking in a way that called or placed the other, but did so in a nongrasping fashion. It was also emphasized that *Nähe* was not a prescription for mystical absorption in being. This last quality finds its parallel in difference feminism's concern that an attitude of care, when properly understood, does not mean that one becomes absorbed in the other, that is, becomes "selfless."[17] This is the most characteristic "potential error in care reasoning," an error that was all too clearly embedded within the traditional ideal of "feminine" virtues. Selflessness in this sense is inextricable from subordination. Although selflessness may be at times one of the most admirable moral virtues, it cannot dominate our image of moral maturity.[18]

Thus the idea of care seems to entail a structure similar to *Nähe*'s play of nearness and distance. In both cases, human beings' participation in being means a placing or bringing forth into language; but that participation becomes distorted when this placing is a grasping and seizing of what is other or distant. Then that participation becomes more like a declaration of the right of mastery, implying an infinitizing urge to control. The mirror image distortion occurs when participation becomes ab-

---

15 Sara Ruddick, "Remarks on the Sexual Politics of Reason," in Kittay and Meyers, *Women and Moral Theory*, pp. 244–5.

16 Ruddick, "Maternal Thinking," p. 350; Gilligan, *In a Different Voice*, p. 57.

17 Gilligan, "Moral Orientation and Moral Development," in Kittay and Meyers, *Women and Moral Theory*, p. 31.

18 Gilligan, *In a Different Voice*, esp. chs. 3 and 5.

sorption, and the terms of relationship collapse into a "speech-less" subordination.

In discussing other thinking and its associated experiences, I drew attention to the moods Heidegger felt could sustain them — "grieving joy" and "shyness" or "awe" — and how the hallmark of such moods is their ambiguity; they embody feelings that pull against one another, that attract one to their object and yet also hold one back. A similar alloy of moods was also found in Derrida's and Lyotard's focus on the sublime. In difference feminism one finds something comparable. Attentive care, according to Ruddick, must be sustained by an alloy of "resilient good humor and humility." The humility here is not specific in its focus, but rather is again a basic attitude "toward a world beyond one's control"; it "accepts not only the facts of damage and death, but also the facts of the independent and uncontrollable, developing and . . . separate existences of the lives it seeks to preserve." But the current of grief and melancholy implied in this sensitivity crosses another current: that of a resilient cheer-fulness that accepts the fragility and mutability of oneself, the world, and the others toward whom one exercises care.[19] This *Stimmung* in which the currents of delight and humility mingle and pull against one another is the deepest motivational re-source for keeping the attitude of care held between the poles of dominating the other and succumbing to him or her.

The foregoing affinities of measure and mood between feminist thinking and that of Heidegger and postmodernism should help clarify why it makes little sense to think of an orientation toward care as simply a women's morality. Moreover, the contextualization of care within the framework of the two senses of responsibility can help disentangle the question of whether two alternative, self-sufficient accounts of the ethical domain can be given, one couched in the language of care, the other in the language of justice. Gilligan suggests this, at least implicitly, with her demarcation of two ethics; and yet her underlying plea is for a vision of contemporary morality in which a conscious experiencing of the tension between the two becomes a hallmark of mature judgment.[20] When one thinks in terms of the two horizons of responsibility, one can understand why, on the one hand, femi-

19 Ruddick, "Maternal Thinking," pp. 350–2.
20 Gilligan, *In a Different Voice*, Ch. 6. These issues are also discussed in a number of the essays in Kittay and Meyers, *Women and Moral Theory*.

nists have strongly emphasized the distinctiveness of the position they have been articulating. Theirs is not an insight that is easily folded into or explained away by, say, contractarian views. And yet, on the other hand, that does not imply that the perspective of care is an alternative, self-sufficient account of the ethical domain. Any given general account of the ethical domain will involve some sensitivity to both senses of responsibility. The emphasis on care then becomes a plea to realign modern sensitivity in a fundamental way, that is, in a way that adequately recognizes the different gravitational field of a responsibility to otherness – a pull on our existence that is rooted finally in the fact of finitude.

II. From the intimate to the ethical–political

If the foregoing contextualization of the care perspective is plausible, then the question Gilligan ends her book with is broadly the same as the one I have been pursuing throughout this book: How do we put the two responsibilities into a creative tension that will shed new light on ethics and politics against the background of the postmodern problematic? Thus it is helpful to examine feminist efforts to envision a more fruitful relationship between the horizon of care and that of traditional theories of justice. And here an issue of crucial significance is how well it can be demonstrated that the former really has implications that go beyond ethical concerns specific to intimate relationships.[21]

A perceptive effort to make some progress on these matters comes from Seyla Benhabib, who tries to supplement a Habermasian communicative ethics with the insights of difference feminism. She begins by developing a critique of something common to different ethics of justice such as Rawls's. They all conceptualize the moral point of view as that of a disembodied, decontextualized "generalized other" – for example, the person imagined under Rawls's "veil of ignorance."[22] One is supposed to assume this point of view when deciding what is right in relations between oneself and other individuals. Building upon earlier

21 See Kohlberg's criticisms of Gilligan in "Synopses and Detailed Replies to Critics," with Charles Levine and Alexandra Hewer, in Lawrence Kohlberg, *Essays on Moral Development*, Vol. II, *The Psychology of Moral Development* (San Francisco: Harper and Row, 1984), pp. 229–30, 360.
22 Seyla Benhabib, "The Generalized and the Concrete Other: The Kohlberg–Gilligan Controversy and Feminist Theory," in *Praxis International* 5 (January 1986), pp. 402–24.

critiques of this way of thinking about justice that question the very possibility of conceiving of selves apart from substantial, concrete knowledge about them, Benhabib argues that one cannot carry out a universalizability test adequately from the point of view of the generalized other. This test, in some form, is the heart of an ethic of justice, and it presupposes that "like cases ought to be treated alike." But we cannot really distinguish "like" and "unlike" situations as they appear to *different, concrete* individuals when we take the standpoint of the homogeneous, generalized other. Benhabib thus concludes that "no coherent universalizability test can be carried out" from such a standpoint.[23]

Either the standpoint of the generalized other is completely empty or its content implicitly identifies "the experience of a specific group of subjects as the paradigmatic case of the human as such."[24] There is thus a prejudged identity of all subjects at the very start of moral argument. For those who share this model of identity, the structure for the ensuing argumentation may be perfectly fair. However, Benhabib and other critics of traditional variants of moral universalism suggest that the structure may be blindly biased against others for whom that model is at least partly inappropriate. Benhabib does not, as a consequence, reject universalism in toto; rather, she suggests that we must think in terms of a "dialogic interactive generation of universality."[25] This would mean that principles and norms claiming universal status would have to be much more fallibly proffered in terms of sensitivity to actual differences between subjects.

One can do justice to this deepened concern for otherness, Benhabib argues, only if we take more seriously a different way of conceptualizing the moral point of view. One must think not only in terms of some interpretation of the generalized other, but also in terms of the standpoint of the "concrete other." From this point of view, one focuses not on commonality but on difference. One is attentive to the other's "concrete history, identity, and affective-emotional constitution," so that she "feels recognized, and confirmed as a concrete, individual being with specific needs, talents, and capacities."[26]

The standpoint of the concrete other is usually associated with

23 Benhabib, "The Generalized and the Concrete Other," pp. 414–15.
24 Ibid., p. 406.
25 Ibid., p. 416.
26 Ibid., pp. 410–11, 416.

the deeply caring attitude of intimate relations between lovers and friends. But, for Benhabib, such an attitude must be brought to bear on questions such as justice. Our ethical–political life must be rethought in a way that "acknowledges that every generalized other is also a concrete other." Only by consistently keeping the latter standpoint in mind will one be forced to confront the "*ideological* limits" of traditional universalist moral theories. The concrete other "signifies the *unthought*, the *unseen*, and the *unheard* in such theories."[27]

I find Benhabib's critique of traditional moral universalism persuasive, but the use she makes of care raises at least as many questions as it answers. Two of these have broad significance. I suggest that the difficulties Benhabib encounters could be alleviated if the tension between justice and care were rethought within the framework of the two senses of responsibility.

A

Benhabib envisions the standpoint of the concrete other as injecting an "anticipatory–utopian" dimension into moral discourse. The narrow focus on norms of justice can now be broadened to include questions of the good life or good society. Discourse now continually taps into "intimations of otherness" that emerge when an attitude of care is brought into play and previously "private" needs, motives, desires, and so on are made accessible to moral communication.[28]

Now Benhabib is right to emphasize how a fine-grained attention to concrete others can broaden the range of possibility within which we can reflect upon the good life. But in framing the issues as she does, she embeds a problem within her perspective. When she endorses the standpoint of the concrete other as adopted in intimate relationships, she implicitly accepts the intensity of care and of mutual expectation that is typical of such relationships. When that intensity is joined to her anticipatory–utopian orientation, one is hard pressed not to envision a society in which the bonds of community may be tied extremely tightly. Benhabib senses this kind of danger and asserts that she is not suggesting that some particular conception of the good life "ei-

27 Ibid.
28 Ibid., pp. 416–18.

ther *can* or *should be* universalized."[29] Although this disclaimer is admirable, the tide generated by her ethical–political vision seems to run in a contrary direction. If this is so, then Benhabib has repeated a gesture for which critics have often rebuked feminists: implicitly extending the promise of a warmer, more deeply satisfying communal life without adequately illustrating why it would not corrode the commitment to diversity and difference.

Perhaps if the concern for concrete others is rethought within the additional contexts I have considered in the preceding chapters, then better support can be given for the sorts of limitations Benhabib explicitly wants on the claims of community. The idea of a lighter care than that appropriate to intense, intimate relationships would relieve her vision of the implicit threat of communal suffocation. The profile of this lighter care would, as I have suggested, share the mood and measure of more intense care; but its distinctiveness and palpability would not be directly anchored in the needs and motivations of intimate relations, but rather in the needs and motivations that are forming in the context of our frustrations and dissatisfactions with modernity.

B

Another set of concerns with Benhabib's appropriation of the perspective of care emerges in a critique by Nancy Fraser. She applauds the reorientation to concreteness but questions whether its close connection to care in intimate relations robs it of any plausible ethical–political implications. An intense concern for the unique life history of each *individual* is largely out of place in the world of politics. In a sense, Benhabib has misplaced the emphasis on concreteness. For ethical–political life, we must attend to the *collective* level. Fraser's proposal is to thematize the standpoint of the "*collective concrete other*." When this is done, we have abstracted "*both* from unique individuality *and* from universal humanity to focalize the intermediate zone of group identity." And this, in turn, eventuates not in "an ethic of care and responsibility" but rather in an "*ethic of solidarity*." Only the latter will be adequately "attuned to the contestatory activities of social movements struggling to forge narrative resources and vocabularies adequate to their self-interpreted needs," while at the same time

29 Ibid., p. 418.

struggling "to deconstruct" the pretensions of "narrative forms and vocabularies of dominant groups and collectivities."[30]

From the point of view of the postmodern problematic, Fraser's criticism seems quite promising. It is well adapted to the issues raised by new social movements, and it thematizes informational technology and communication structures from the viewpoints of domination and empowerment. Moreover, it remains tied to communicative ethics and its minimal, universalistic approach to justice. This is crucial, because too often the focus of postmodern thinkers on informationalization and the "new pluralism" comes at the cost of extraordinary confusion over what to do about claims of justice. (I will have much more to say about this in the next chapter.) What concerns me at this point, however, is whether Fraser too quickly abandons the notion of care, severing cleanly the ties – which I have traced through Heidegger and difference feminism – between it and the notion of concreteness or particularity.

The costs of this abandonment are not insignificant. Fraser's standpoint of the collective concrete other fosters an intensification of specific group identity and commitment to norms of solidarity within that group. Moreover, the most "privileged moral feeling" would be that associated with the bonds of solidarity.[31] My concern is that Fraser is perhaps a little insensitive to how much the notion of solidarity here is likely to be bound up with strong negative perceptions of those others *against* whom one defines oneself. Perhaps in the worst sorts of political circumstances, such an emphasis is acceptable because it is necessary. But politics in postmodern society would not seem to fit this profile much of the time.

Fraser counters here that the feeling of unalloyed group struggle will be tempered by the reciprocity requirement implied in the standpoint of the concrete other: "We owe each other behavior such that each is confirmed as a being with specific collective identifications and solidarities."[32] Presumably this would mean protection of the autonomy of different groups and an attitude of tolerance. Although I find that this line of thinking lays out important minimal ethical–political criteria, I question whether

30 Nancy Fraser, "Toward a Discourse Ethic of Solidarity," *Praxis International* 5 (January 1986), pp. 427–9.
31 Ibid., p. 428.
32 Ibid.

the perspective as a whole does not still remain too strongly dominated by the ideals of collectivity and struggle against other collectivities. Strong echoes remain of some of the most questionable orientations of modern thought: struggle against the other subject and struggle against nature. Perhaps an agonistic orientation toward collective others, tempered by tolerance, does represent an advance in some ways, but is it really reflective enough about these echoes?

Such problems can be avoided, while at the same time preserving some of Fraser's insights, if the connection between concreteness and care is not so cleanly severed. When care is interpreted in the lighter way I have been suggesting, there are fewer grounds for the sort of skepticism Fraser expresses. The real proof of the pudding, however, will, of course, be found in the ways such a perspective on care can actually inform ethical–political life. This task will not be well conceived if one thinks in terms of constructing some grand alternative model of politics. Rather, one should think more in terms of modes of counterpoint to the dominant patterns of interaction. The point of such modes would be the continual infusion of these patterns with the theme of otherness and finitude.

A useful way into the whole question of ethical–political implications is to consider what might be called the "threshold" issue. By this I mean the fact that a wide range of theorists have focused upon political life below, or at, the threshold of what is normally considered organized politics and administration. For example, feminists worry about large-scale organizations routinizing and normalizing the more radical impulses that were sustained in smaller, consciousness-raising groups.[33] Habermas sees the state and formal party organizations as structured in such a way as to promote the "colonization of the lifeworld." Thus, he focuses attention on reconceptualizing public spheres as functioning below the threshold where the systemic imperatives of power and money become so dominant.[34] And, finally, in Foucault a similar pattern of concern emerges, although he is –

---

33 See Ferguson, *The Feminist Case against Bureaucracy,* and Jane Mansbridge, "Feminism and the Forms of Freedom," in Frank Fischer and Carmen Sirianni, eds., *Organization and Bureaucracy* (Philadelphia: Temple University Press, 1984), pp. 472–81.

34 Habermas, *The Philosophical Discourse of Modernity: Twelve Lectures,* trans. by Frederick Lawrence (Cambridge, Mass.: MIT Press, 1987), pp. 362–5.

typically – less explicit and more ambivalent. Impulses for a healthier politics are located below, or at least on the borders of, normalized social and political life: in "subjugated knowledges" and local resistance that constitute friction points for the expansion of "disciplinary" apparatuses.[35]

Despite differences in the way the threshold issue is conceptualized, what remains common is the concern to preserve public breathing spaces for discourses that are "abnormal" from the viewpoint of societal rationalization. Now what exactly constitutes "abnormality" is, of course, a matter of dispute. But it is precisely here that the orientation to care as I have elaborated it might be brought to bear. It could provide a way of partially constituting the meaning of such alternative discourse or interaction that supplements other ways recently suggested. It will, first, cut deeper into modern prejudices than Habermas's idea of unconstrained communicative action. It will also cut deeper than Rorty's notion of abnormal discourse, which critics have seen as folding all too easily into the normality of Western society.[36] And it will cut differently (at least partially) than the discourse of French postmodernism for all the reasons I have previously laid out. And, finally, it will cut differently from difference feminism, at least insofar as that mode of thought has been unable to shed the persistent criticism that it applies only to the sphere of intimate relations.

From the perspective of the two senses of responsibility, the notion of public interactions "below the threshold" can be construed as modes of intersubjectivity in which the two senses play back and forth upon one another. More particularly, the responsibility to act is not allowed to displace radically the responsibility to otherness. Here the issue is – as Benhabib and Frazer correctly

---

35 Foucault, *Power/Knowledge: Selected Interviews and Other Writings* (New York: Pantheon, 1972), pp. 81–5; *History of Sexuality*, Vol. 1: *An Introduction* (New York: Random House, 1980), pp. 95–96.

36 See the critiques of Rorty by William Connolly, "The Mirror of America," *Raritan* (Summer 1983), reprinted in Connolly, *Politics and Ambiguity* (Madison: University of Wisconsin Press, 1987), pp. 116–26, and Richard Bernstein, "One Step Forward, Two Steps Backward: Richard Rorty on Liberal Democracy and Philosophy," *Political Theory* 15, no. 4 (November 1987), pp. 538–63. The term "abnormal" discourse is used by Richard Rorty, *Philosophy and the Mirror of Nature* (Princeton, N.J.: Princeton University Press, 1979), pp. 320ff. See the discussion by Fred Dallmayr, "Conversation, Discourse, and Politics," in *Polis and Praxis: Exercises in Contemporary Political Theory* (Cambridge, Mass.: MIT Press, 1984), pp. 192–223.

see – one of constituting modes of intersubjectivity that confirm the concrete other. But, as I have tried to show, their approaches misconceive that task. In order to help establish the distinctiveness of my approach, a restatement of their drawbacks – with a slightly different emphasis – may be helpful. Benhabib ties the task of confirming the concrete other too closely to the model of care in intimate relations, thereby infecting it with a centripetal emotional intensity that threatens public interactions with communal suffocation. Fraser avoids the gravitational pull of such emotion by dropping the emphasis on care altogether, replacing it with the value of solidarity within a collective. But, as I have suggested, the task of confirming the concrete other here seems destined to undermine itself again as the centripetal emotions associated with the solidarity of an "us" blunt our sensitivity to "them." Although the motivational power of such internal solidarity is supposed to be balanced by the countervailing commitment to reciprocal respect *between* collectivities, the latter seems to have such an affective thinness to it that it would fall prey all too easily to the force of solidarity.

In sum, both Benhabib and Fraser find the motivating force of an affective orientation crucial to the task of confirming the concrete other, but they fail to articulate such an orientation in a way that will sustain the sort of ethical–political interaction they wish to foster. As feminists, both share a deep dissatisfaction and frustration with the imperatives of modern life. The approach I am suggesting emerges from a broadly similar dissatisfaction and frustration, but it is tied to the cultivation of a mood that might sustain modes of ethical–political interaction within which the embrace of an us is not too tight and the distance from a them does not harbor a propensity to hostility.[37]

Confirming the concrete other is now an activity tuned by the sort of affective orientation suggested by Heidegger and Ruddick. The cultivation of a mood of "grieving delight" might give us greater sensitivity to the dangers of suffocating others whom we identify as part of an us, as well as to the dangers of attitudes

---

37 At times Heidegger drew a sharp distinction between "moods" [*Stimmungen*] and "feelings" [*Gefühle*]. A key aspect of moods is that we do not control them; in a sense, "they have us, we don't have them." Feelings, on the other hand, were for Heidegger more manipulable and superficial; they had a pedestrian quality. I would suggest that this distinction is vastly overdrawn and reflects Heidegger's mandarin tendencies. Moods can be cultivated or discouraged by behavior. Thoreau seems to have done just this.

that help give us an identity whose potency feeds implicitly off the denigration of a them. This mood and its measure of *Nähe* might embed in our practice a basic commitment to listening to otherness – in us or them. This listening would be guided by a wariness of too quickly freezing the other's story into one's own stock of familiar interpretive frames. One's listening would try to hold the narrative between self and other, let it play back and forth between the terms of one's own interpretive frames and those of the other, thereby recognizing the twin dangers of dominating the other and simply submitting to her or his terms.

By cultivating the mood and measure that sustain such a listening, we begin to become at home in homelessness: in finitude, in radical contingency, in a world that continually pushes over, edges around, and seeps through our attempts to freeze it within frames of interpretation. This mood carries within it an indissoluble ambiguity. First, there is mournfulness and grief at the fragility and momentary quality of all that we value and affirm. It is out of this affective pole that we might come to a greater sense of the tragic dimension of political life. But at the same time there is the sense of delight in the continual presencing of difference, of the other. It is out of this affective pole that we might be motivated toward ways of responding to the other in political life that go beyond simple tolerance, without, however, sliding into paternalism.[38]

The positive valuation of difference, as opposed to mere tolerance, could give us grounds for a stronger commitment to public policies that do not merely *protect* the formal right of individual or collective concrete others to express themselves, but go further and do more to *empower* or to *foster* the emergence of such voices. In its broadest sense, this notion could be joined with calls for greater "*slack* or space within modern institutions" that have come from a Foucauldian direction.[39] Such a call entails greater rethinking of such institutions than the traditional liberal call for tolerance, because the reach and inconspicuousness of the infinite urge to discipline life are more extreme than the dangers recognized by liberal thought. (I expand on this and some of the following points in Chapter 7.)

38 See the interesting insights in Dallmayr, "Conversation, Discourse, and Politics," *Polis and Praxis*.
39 William Connolly, "Discipline, Politics and Ambiguity" *Political Theory* 11 (August 1983), p. 337. Reprinted in Connolly, *Politics and Ambiguity*.

More specifically, this sort of positive evaluation of difference would require a thorough reconsideration of how what Fraser calls "the socio-cultural means of interpretation and communication" could be arranged and their control distributed in such a way that social movements could more easily "forge [the] narrative resources and vocabularies adequate to the expression of their self-interpreted needs."[40] Here one can relocate the value of Fraser's points about confirming the collective concrete other without severing them from a perspective of care. The emergence of new technologies of communication and information not only makes this problem more pressing but also allows perhaps for more unorthodox attempts to confront it.

Benhabib's point about utopia and otherness can now also be reappropriated. The positive valuation of difference implies a continual openness toward utopian intimations, a continual leavening of our fixed frames of reference. The perspective offered here keeps this openness from being bundled up into the notion that these intimations are collectable into a utopian, communal *vision of society* that needs only to be implemented. Here one can begin to see the effect of that other dimension of the mood that should orient the responsibility to otherness: grief, mournfulness, and humility. These feelings should be a subtle but constant companion as we fulfill our responsibility to act. However, their effect should be especially clear in relation to the problem of deflating grand schemes for the implementation of utopian blueprints of political life.

Another way in which this dimension of grief and humility might be seen to have political effects is in the way it could orient one toward remembering or commemorating the fate of concrete others in political life. This feeling would work to sensitize one continually to the inevitable, tragic dimension of politics. The cognitive machinery of modern politics too often neutralizes this dimension totally or reinterprets what is involved as "costs" within a calculus of action.

To be more specific, the grief and humility of a postmodern mood could be a source of orientation for the sort of political action sometimes endorsed by difference feminists. Jean Elshtain has offered Antigone as the exemplar of a challenge to the

40 Fraser, "Toward a Discourse Ethic of Solidarity," p. 428.

political system grounded in the exigencies of family life.[41] This
is a challenge that resists the overriding and forgetting of the
concrete other, in this case Antigone's brother and the need to
bury him. Now commemorating the concrete other is not something entirely foreign to the established agendas of modern political systems. But the others are typically a privileged class:
primarily "forefathers" and heroic war dead. Implicit in Elshtain's argument is a plea that commemoration be extended
through public action to the suffering of unofficial, unprivileged
others.

Like most difference feminists, Elshtain has been subjected to
heavy critical fire, in her case for tying the politics of women too
closely to the model of Antigone.[42] The model might be interpreted as implying that women should focus only on family issues in politics, and do so only in extraordinary situations.
Elshtain has argued that this interpretation is incorrect; her aim
is to draw attention to the exemplar of Antigone in order to
speculate about how a perspective of care might become a "wider
social imperative."[43] The broader implications of Elshtain's argument are more apparent in a contemporary case she has analyzed: the so-called Mothers of the Plaza de Mayos in Argentina,
whose persistent demonstrations against the military regime's
systematic, covert killing of civilians was an important element in
the reemergence of democracy in that country. Here the collective, cooperative, and linguistic character of the exemplar has
powerful political implications. Individual, family grief opened
onto a broader dimension. As Elshtain puts it:

> The language [the Mothers] spoke was double: the language of a
> mother's loss and the language of human rights, moving from
> intensely particular, yet universally recognized, imperatives of
> love and terror, to what has become a universal and potent politi-
> cal discourse.[44]

41 Elshtain, "Antigone's Daughters"; and "Antigone's Daughters Reconsidered:
Continuing Reflections on Women, Politics and Power," in Stephen K. White,
ed., *Lifeworld and Politics: Between Modernity and Postmodernity, Essays in Honor of
Fred Dallmayr* (Notre Dame, Ind.: University of Notre Dame Press, 1989), pp.
222–35.
42 See some of the literature cited in the notes of Elshtain, "Antigone's Daughters Reconsidered."
43 Elshtain, "Antigone's Daughters," p. 59.
44 Elshtain, "Antigone's Daughters Reconsidered," p. 232.

It is these sorts of interconnections between levels of discourse and feeling that a postmodern affective orientation might also foster. In this sense, the effort to bring the results of reflections on postmodernity and otherness into play complements the insights Elshtain has developed. However, the former locates these insights less predominantly in the family. The frustration, the dissatisfaction, and the (hopefully) emergent mood are phenomena rooted in all sorts of everyday lifeworld experiences in modern society. In this regard, one of the most attractive features of Foucault and Derrida is their attempt to think about imaginative, unorthodox ways to remember the unofficial, unprivileged concrete other. Although there is much that is problematic about this thinking, as I have shown, its deepest roots do indeed seem to be sunk in a soil where grief and the urge to respond to the other's daily suffering are blended.[45]

45 See Derrida, "Racism's Last Word," trans. by Peggy Kamuf, *Critical Inquiry* 12 (Autumn 1985), pp. 290–9, esp. pp. 293–9. Foucault's thinking on these matters is elucidated by Tom Keenan, "The 'Paradox' of Knowledge and Power: Reading Foucault on a Bias," *Political Theory* 15 (February 1987), pp. 19–23.

7

RETHINKING JUSTICE

So far, I have tried to lay out a broad perspective from which one can understand the controversy over postmodernism. My intention has been to find a way of allowing the tension between the antagonists to express itself in an enlivening rather than a repetitive, deadening fashion. In the last chapter I alluded to some of the ways in which this perspective might begin reorienting ethical–political thinking. In order to move beyond such general allusions, however, one must systematically explore what the perspective implies for basic political concepts. Part of this effort, of course, requires attending specifically to how such rethinking confronts the different elements of the postmodern problematic: incredulity toward metanarratives, growing awareness of the costs of societal rationalization, informationalization, and the rise of new social movements. In this chapter I undertake a preliminary exploration of the concept of justice. Implicit in this analysis is the suggestion that parallel investigations into other concepts might lead to similar reorientations.

Why start with justice? There is no necessary reason, but there is a strong one. The overall challenge of postmodern thinking might be rendered into the assertion that we are far too ready to attach the adjective "just" to cognitive, ethical, and political arrangements that are better understood as phenomena of power that oppress, neglect, marginalize, and discipline others. In unmasking such claims about justice, postmodern thinkers imply that their work serves some more valid but unspecific notion of justice. One sees this in Derrida's declaration that "Deconstruction is justice," but also in his cautioning that one can neither speak directly about nor experience justice.[1] In answering the sense of responsibility to otherness, one serves justice but one does so with a sense of the infinite, open-ended character of the task. Responsibility in this sense can never be reduced to conformity with a closed set of rules or principles for guiding action and constructing institutions.

Derrida, as usual, makes his point as provocatively as possible. But, after the effect wears off, one is left with a rather simple bipolar world: deconstructionists and other postmoderns who struggle for justice, and traditional ethical and political theorists who are the ideologues of unjust orders. There is nothing here but two intellectually armed camps. Is it possible to recast the issues so that the tension expresses itself more fruitfully? This possibility, as well as much of Derrida's own intent, seems to be captured in Lyotard's way of phrasing the dilemma. It is necessary, he argues, to develop a perspective "that would respect both the desire for justice and the desire for the unknown" – that would respect the responsibility to act in a normatively justifiable way as well as the responsibility to otherness.[2]

Lyotard's specific contribution to this task will be taken up in a moment. Initially, however, I want to keep the focus as broad as possible, highlighting the relationship of justice to the different components of the postmodern problematic. The task to be faced, stated in its most general terms, is to conceptualize justice in such a way that it takes account of this problematic, as well as the underlying concern with otherness, and yet still articulates our most reflective moral judgments at least as well as the best of more traditional theories of justice. My goal in this chapter is to provide some general sense of what this would involve.

I suggest, first, that justice has to be reconceptualized in a

---

1 Jacques Derrida, "Force of Law: The 'Mystical Foundation of Authority'," paper presented to a conference on "Deconstruction and the Possibility of Justice" at the Cardozo School of Law, New York City, November 1989.
2 Jean-François Lyotard, *The Postmodern Condition: A Report on Knowledge*, trans. by G. Bennington and B. Massumi (Minneapolis: University of Minnesota Press, 1984), p. 67; see Lyotard and Jean-Loup Thébaud, *Just Gaming*, trans. by Wlad Godzich (Minneapolis: University of Minnesota Press, 1985), p. 100.

more deeply pluralist fashion than traditionally has been the case (Section I). Here postmodern thinkers are suggesting a perspective that overlaps with those who would describe themselves as merely "postmetaphysical," such as Michael Walzer. While noting this similarity, some important differences will be stressed that relate to how seriously one confronts the postmodern problematic. A new pluralist reconceptualization of justice, attuned to this problematic, ought to proceed in two directions. First, there must be a more direct focus on the phenomena of *in*justice, rather than thinking of them as merely derivative of justice and thus of only secondary importance (Section II). Second, the issue of *fostering* otherness must become as important as that of *tolerating* otherness. But, at the same time, this more celebratory attitude must be joined with arguments about when it is legitimate to constrain otherness (a task from which postmodern thinkers have tended to shy away) (Section III).

I. A new pluralist justice

If one asks about how the growing incredulity toward foundationalist metanarratives affects the concept of justice, it is important to emphasize that this is not just an issue for those who define themselves as postmodern. Many who are quite skeptical of postmodernist thinking nevertheless share this incredulity. One such postmetaphysical thinker, Michael Walzer, has provided perhaps the most substantial contribution so far to rethinking justice in a more deeply pluralist fashion in his *Spheres of Justice*.[3] Given the fact that Walzer has elaborated his account with more care than any postmodern thinker, it is useful to turn to him for some initial bearings. A more explicitly postmodern perspective will emerge in the course of the discussion, as the rethinking of justice is brought into confrontation with the other aspects of the postmodern problematic.

In order to help establish the legitimacy of focusing upon Walzer in this context, it is useful to elucidate some of the strong similarities between his project and that sketched by Lyotard in *The Postmodern Condition* and *Just Gaming*.[4] Both define themselves in opposition to traditional theories of justice. Such theories are

3 Michael Walzer, *Spheres of Justice: A Defense of Pluralism and Equality* (New York: Basic Books, 1983).
4 See n. 2.

seen as being tied to metanarratives that anchor them philosophically and give them a claim to universal validity. For present purposes, the most important of these are the liberal and Marxian
perspectives. The former grounds justice in quasi-Kantian assumptions about individuals and "primary goods," and the latter
grounds it in assumptions about history and emancipation.

Both Lyotard and Walzer react against the totalizing effect of
metanarratives of justice, that is, the subordination of plurality
and heterogeneity to unity and homogeneity under the regime
of some purportedly universal principles of justice. Both seek a
new account of pluralism that shows the illegitimacy of such a
position.[5] What makes this a new account are two things. First,
pluralism, as it is traditionally understood in liberal thought,
puts a strong emphasis on the sovereign individual. The individual chooses his or her own gods or goods and then may join
groups to pursue them. The new pluralists stress to a much
greater degree the social dimension. Gods and goods have coherent meaning only within a social context. This does not mean a
denigration of the individual, but only an insistence on his or her
embeddedness. The primary focus thus is on the plurality of
meanings goods have across and within cultures (Walzer) or the
plurality of narratives and language games (Lyotard). Second,
this new pluralism emphasizes that a crucial part of doing justice
is "listening" – moving away from the fixation with authoring
determinate principles and toward procedures attuned to recognizing the "boundaries" of a heterogeneous world.[6] In this sense,
Walzer and Lyotard are both strongly committed to developing a
notion of justice that is more open to otherness. Here the contrast with traditional views of justice can be described as one
between approaches that are more strongly attuned to a sense of
responsibility to otherness versus ones attuned primarily to a
responsibility to act, or, more specifically in this case, a responsi-

5 See Fred Dallmayr's discussion of a new pluralism in "Democracy and Postmodernism," *Human Studies* 10, no. 1 (1986), pp. 144, 163–7.
6 Walzer, *Spheres of Justice*, pp. xiv, 4–10, 26–30, 312–21; and Lyotard and
Thébaud, *Just Gaming*, pp. 58–9, 71–2, 87–8. Here I am interested in the
broad philosophical point Walzer is making about moral pluralism in *Spheres of
Justice*. This defines his general position over against, say, Rawls's in *A Theory of
Justice*. I am not concerned with the *specific* thesis Walzer advances about the
high degree of agreement "latent already . . . in our shared understanding of
social goods" (p. xiv). That thesis is more contestable and probably a lot more
unpalatable to someone like Lyotard.

bility to author determinate and unambiguous principles for judgment and action.

The differences between a view like Walzer's and one like Lyotard's begin to emerge when one moves beyond common epistemological concerns to ask about the practical impetus for rethinking justice. In one broad sense there is still some similarity. Just as in Lyotard, Walzer's emphasis on listening, boundaries, and otherness at least partially reflects a general concern about Western cultural imperialism. This is evident in his frequent recourse to non-Western and premodern anthropological sources.[7] And yet in a more explicit sense, Walzer draws justification from the way his approach provides defenses against phenomena associated with twentieth-century totalitarianism. A totalitarian society is the polar opposite of a society respecting boundaries between different spheres of life.[8] Walzer is no doubt right about this in a general sense, but the question I want to raise is whether invoking the specter of the classical totalitarian party-state adequately illuminates the dilemmas of justice in contemporary Western societies. Here thinkers struggling with the full spectrum of the postmodern problematic are providing better insight. Totalitarianism and Western cultural imperialism are, of course, seen by them as dangers; but at the same time, they are attempting to grasp social and political phenomena that are not adequately comprehended by these concepts. They are concerned with a systemic, rationalizing process within Western societies, the effects of which threaten precisely the kinds of values Walzer wants to see protected.

Concern with processes of societal rationalization can be traced back to Marx and Max Weber. Theorists attuned to the postmodern problematic depart sharply, however, from Marx. As emphasized earlier, they reject any solution to this rationalization envisioned in the form of a totalistic revolutionary program. Moreover, they are critical of Marx's legacy for socialists in general who have intensely analyzed disempowerment in the economic sphere but have failed to understand the depth of this problem in the political sphere of large, complex societies. These theorists are much closer to Weber in their appreciation of the ambiguous and paradoxical qualities of modern life and

7 Walzer, *Spheres of Justice*, p. xviii.
8 Ibid., pp. 315–17.

in their lack of programmatic optimism. But postmodern reflection on societal rationalization also departs from Weber in significant ways. Two of these are particularly important in the present context. An illumination of these contrasts will help locate ways in which postmodern reflection on justice needs to go beyond a perspective such as Walzer's.

The first difference is most evident in the work of Foucault. His analysis of the normalizing logic of modern life looks beyond Weber's concern for the individual subject's freedom in a world increasingly dominated by rational–legal authority; it goes further and finds that our very conceptions of subjectivity are themselves already deeply structured by processes of power. And these processes are inextricably related to the generation of knowledge in the human sciences, as Foucault's analyses of punishment and sexuality have shown. What this means is that the logic of societal rationalization in modern life penetrates the consciousness and behavior of individuals more deeply than Weber imagined, and that the growing informationalization of society is only likely to make this problem more acute. We are bathed in an increasing volume of information that is continually coded and recoded to meet the interests of corporate capitalism and public administration; and in this process our traditions, expectations, and consciousness of who we are are deeply structured.

If these theorists are correct, this has distinct implications for the new pluralist approach to justice, for societal rationalization in an age of informationalization threatens otherness and the autonomy of different spheres of meaning in new and subtle ways. It does so because the dominant discourses and institutions that carry rationalization processes forward so structure public meanings and social relationships that alternative discourses and forms of life find critical footholds difficult to secure.[9] What this means is that openness to the continual emergence of otherness is under a systematic threat that Walzer does not bring into the foreground of his reflections in *Spheres of Justice*.

A second way in which postmodern reflection on rationalization and informationalization differs from Weber relates to the topic of legitimacy and authority. Weber's logic of legitimacy involves rational–legal authority increasingly displacing tradi-

9 See Jürgen Habermas, *The Theory of Communicative Action*, Vol. 2, *Lifeworld and System*, trans. by Thomas A. McCarthy (Boston: Beacon Press, 1987), pp. 325–7, 355–6.

tional and charismatic authority.[10] In framing the problem this way, Weber establishes the parameters of a social world in which otherness will increasingly be cornered in shrinking spheres of localized traditional life or burst out sporadically in charismatic movements.

From this perspective, if one tries to interpret the phenomena of "postmaterial values" and "new social movements," one is bound to see them as some sort of manifestation of charisma. But this hardly seems a fruitful category of analysis.[11] It is at this impasse that theorists wrestling with the postmodern problematic hope to explore some new normative horizons. Broadly speaking, this involves reconsidering how we think about the relationship between familiar or dominant discourses and abnormal ones. And a crucial part of this effort is greater attention to the threshold I discussed in the last chapter between, on the one hand, the money- and power-driven institutions of economic and administrative–political life, and, on the other hand, less formally structured modes of public interaction.

This nexus of questions provides a common focus for the normative reflections of a range of thinkers from Foucault to Lyotard to Habermas. These reflections, of course, go off in different directions. Habermas has elaborated a minimal, procedural, discursive conception of justice that is intended to be more open to difference than that of familiar proceduralist conceptions such as John Rawls's or Bruce Ackerman's.[12] I will suggest in a moment that postmodern normative reflection needs such a component; however, as I have emphasized before, Habermas's engagement with the postmodern problematic lacks a deep enough sense of responsibility to otherness to provide by

---

10 Max Weber, *Economy and Society: An Outline of Interpretive Sociology*, ed. by Guenther Roth and Claus Wittich (Berkeley: University of California Press, 1978).

11 Religious fundamentalist groups may be more susceptible to Weberian analysis in terms of the charismatic authority of television evangelists. See Timothy W. Luke, *Screens of Power: Ideology, Domination and Resistance in Informational Society* (Urbana: University of Illinois Press, 1989), ch. 3. They also could be separated from other new social movements on the grounds that they tend to be highly intolerant of diversity in forms of life.

12 For a lucid and persuasive account of the superiority of Habermas's discursive ethics to the proceduralism of Rawls or Ackerman, see Simone Chambers, "Discourse and Procedural Ethics," Ph.D. dissertation, Columbia University, 1990; also my *The Recent Work of Jürgen Habermas: Reason, Justice and Modernity* (Cambridge: Cambridge University Press, 1988), ch. 4.

itself an adequate perspective on justice. In what follows, I want to ask whether such an enlarged perspective can be sketched using resources provided by the French postmoderns and the notion of a lighter care.

Any such attempt must begin by taking seriously the depth of the dilemma that postmodern reflection on ethical–political life has created for itself. On the one hand, its epistemological project is to deflate all totalistic, universalistic efforts to theorize about justice and the good life; and yet, on the other hand, its practical project is to generate effective resistance to the present dangers of totalizing, universalizing rationalization processes in society. In short, the source of much injustice in contemporary society is seen as general and systematic; the response, however, bars itself from normatively confronting the problem on a comparable level by employing a theory of justice offering universally valid, substantive principles. Postmodern reflection thus seems to deny itself just the sort of normative armament capable of conducting a successful fight. What sorts of theoretical strategies relevant to justice might one adopt after having renounced in advance the advantages of a strong substantive theory? In the following sections, I suggest two possibilities.

II. The phenomena of injustice

The first strategy is to begin thinking about injustice in a different way. Judith Shklar (dealing with a set of concerns not directly related to the present ones) has raised the question of injustice as follows:

> Why should we not think of those experiences that we call unjust directly, as independent phenomena in their own right? Common sense and history surely tell us that these are primary experiences and have an immediate claim on our attention. Indeed, most of us in all likelihood have said, "this is unfair or unjust," a lot more often than "this is just." Is there nothing much to be said about the sense of injustice that we know so well when we feel it? Why then do most philosophers refuse to think about injustice as deeply or as subtly as about justice?[13]

13 Judith Shklar, "Giving Injustice Its Due," *Yale Law Journal* 98 (April 1989), p. 1135.

The dominant tradition in philosophy tends to see injustice as a derivative phenomenon: as what happens when just norms are broken. Injustice is not only derivative within this tradition; it is also of secondary concern, because it tends to be seen as essentially correctable, even if rectification comes only in the long run. For these reasons, it is to the question of justice that the dominant tradition directs its theoretical efforts. Justice is the goal; injustices are temporary obstacles.

Shklar's perspective emerges from a countertradition of philosophical skepticism about political life. Here injustice becomes a central and ineliminable feature of the world, because "we simply cannot know enough about men or events to fulfill the demands of justice." The skeptic consistently deflates the dominant model's faith in the efficacy of norms – a faith that feeds a deceptive intellectual self-assurance. The replacing of this faith with a more sustained focus on injustice would promise a finer-grained illumination of neglected ethical–political phenomena, such as the different faces of victimhood and "the many ways in which we all learn to live with each other's injustices."[14] Shklar's ideas are of immediate interest because of the way in which they suggest a plausible, general framework for locating and developing postmodern insights in relation to justice. The suspiciousness of postmodern thinking in regard to traditional political philosophy can now be seen as both partially warranted and yet not radically divorced from all efforts to develop systematic normative discourse.

The most basic practical effect of a more serious thematization of injustice, Shklar argues, would be "an enhanced sense of the dominion of injustice" in human affairs. This is again quite compatible with the various strategies of postmodern thinkers that are designed to unsettle us by showing that domains typically thought of as being ruled by rational norms are in fact shot through with power. Here the qualities of impertinence and hyperbole, on which I have so far largely cast doubt, can take on a positive significance. Foucault's persistent use of metaphors of warfare, for ex-

14 Ibid., pp. 1135–40. The theorists Shklar finds most helpful are Plato, St. Augustine, Cicero, and Montaigne. Foucault has often been associated with the tradition of skepticism. See John Rajchman, *Michel Foucault: The Freedom of Philosophy* (New York: Columbia University Press, 1985), pp. 2, 4. See Richard J. Bernstein, "Foucault: Critique as a Philosophic Ethos," unpublished manuscript, 1988.

ample, promotes a kind of hypersensitivity to power processes. It goads us into considering whether far more phenomena in contemporary society are instances of domination and injustice than would appear to be the case from the perspective of more traditional political theories. Such a theoretical strategy can now be appreciated as an initial means of enhancing sensitivity to the intractability and pervasiveness of injustice. But this strategy has to be joined with some other forms of ethical–political reflection if it is not to become a dead end. The notion of care, as I have elaborated it in conjunction with the mood and measure of a postmodern sensibility, can provide the basis for just such reflection.

In one sense, much of normal interest group politics can be superficially conceptualized as activity to combat injustice. The American steel industry often portrays itself as the victim of injustice at the hands of foreign corporations selling steel in the United States at government-subsidized prices. And on this basis, its lobbying arm appeals to Congress for redress. Now there is hardly any need for new normative perspectives to help highlight such "wrongs." Clearly, a focus on injustice in the present context must imply something more. Toward that end, I want to sketch briefly a way of perceiving the confrontation of public wrongs at a more everyday level. Shklar is again helpful here when she draws upon Cicero's distinction between active and passive injustice. The underlying idea is that a citizen may act unjustly not only by, for example, breaking a law, but also by remaining passive when a public wrong – violence, fraud, suffering, and so on – is perceived and no official agency steps in to remedy the situation. With this notion, one thematizes an area of responsibility that is larger than that of the citizen of a liberal polity who is expected only to refrain from active injustice.[15] This expanded area of responsibility is given its traditional sense in terms of classical republicanism, at the beginning of which Cicero stands. There one finds an emphasis on active citizenship, promotion of the public good, and protection of the bonds of community. One could also easily fit the idea of passive injustice into recent communitarian political thought.[16]

15 Shklar, "Giving Injustice Its Due," pp. 1142–6.
16 Notable communitarians include Alisdair Macintyre, *After Virtue*, 2nd ed. (Notre Dame, Ind.: University of Notre Dame Press, 1984); and Michael Sandel *Liberalism and the Limits of Justice* (Cambridge: Cambridge University Press, 1982).

But, construed in either of these fashions, citizens might be given license to rectify passive injustice in ways that are abusive of deeply held values of modernity. When the primary concern is the cohesiveness of a republic or community, the activism implied in overcoming passive injustice may be easily turned in exclusivist directions or extended in ways that so tighten the bonds of community as to suffocate diversity. One imagines, for example, the citizens of Rousseau's *Social Contract* as being highly sensitive to passive injustice. In a mood of self-righteousness, they would feel amply justified in disciplining groups whose morals or customs were perceived as offensive to community values.

As an alternative, one might think of the problem of passive injustice from the perspective of postmodern care. Here the sense of injustice would not be tuned by the feeling of self-righteousness and the value of communal solidarity, but rather by a subtle grieving for all those who bear the added burden of a life of needless suffering and injustice. Care in this sense does not imply a need to help mold victims in accordance with a set of substantive values. It is adequately expressed, first, by the sensitivity with which one initially comprehends the specific situation of injustice or suffering; and, second, by the alleviation of the particular burdens.

Given these qualities, it would be expected that the most appropriate sites for the expression of this enhanced sense of public obligation are local ones. There the possibilities for understanding and effective citizen action are maximized. The primary focus remains, at least partially, below the threshold where the rationalizing imperatives of large organizations and mass media dominate interaction and understanding. But this focus should not be thought of as exclusive. In a rapidly informationalizing world, a sort of second-level face-to-faceness seems to be emerging that takes place above, as it were, the level of nation-states. Foucault was especially sensitive to this dimension, as evidenced by his activity to aid Vietnamese refugees in the early 1980s. He clearly wanted to emphasize the need for direct citizen response to such suffering in the absence of effective action by nation-states and official international organizations. No doubt he was just as clearly aware of how easily such efforts at an international level could be trivialized by the same mass media that transmitted the vivid images of death and despair in the first place (e.g., in the way television news organizations in the United States easily become bored with the repetition of a story and thus quickly turn to novel sources of vivid images). Foucault attempted to accompany his practical efforts with suggestions for reconceptualizing what was at issue in a normative sense. But he never got much further than appealing, rather opaquely, to a "new form of right."[17] Perhaps by placing his practice within the perspective of care and struggle against passive injustice, one can provide a reconceptualization with which he might not have been uncomfortable.

III. Fostering and constraining otherness

A second strategy in terms of which problems associated with justice can be rethought has to do with supplementing the traditional liberal value of tolerating diversity with the idea of more actively fostering it. Liberal thought has often come in for heavy fire from postmodernists, as well as feminists, for endorsing, explicitly or implicitly, various ways of suppressing or marginalizing difference. Defenders of liberalism counter that perhaps particular formulations are guilty in this regard, but that the liberal tradition in general is best understood precisely as a response to the emergence of moral pluralism as a primary reality of political life in the modern West. This understanding places special emphasis on the principle of toleration.[18] There is much to recommend such an interpretation of liberalism. But the approach I am following does not so much contest this claim as question whether liberal tolerance alone is sufficient for grappling with the problem of difference or otherness in a social world where the pressures of rationalization and informationalization are so insistent.

In order to establish some plausibility for this position, I first elaborate the rationale for supplementing the value of tolerance with an attention to fostering (Subsection A). Then I consider the difficulty many postmodern thinkers have in combining a

17 Michel Foucault, "Two Lectures," in *Power/Knowledge: Selected Interviews and Other Writings, 1972–1977*, ed. by Colin Gordon (New York: Pantheon, 1980), p. 105. For a good overview of Foucault's political activity, see Keith Gandal, "Foucault: Intellectual Work and Politics," *Telos* 67 (Spring 1986), pp. 121–34.
18 See Donald Moon, "Citizenship and Gender," paper presented to the New England Political Science Association, Annual meeting, Portland, Maine, April 1990.

commitment to fostering with at least some minimal criteria of normative constraint on what gets fostered. One of the often heard broadsides against postmodernism is that it amounts to nothing more than an endorsement of "anything goes." With this is mind, I examine and criticize Lyotard's conceptualization of fostering and constraint (Subsection B). Finally, I take up the question of how the liberal notion of the neutral state must be modified in order to take into account adequately the problem of justice and otherness (Subsection C).

A

The principle of toleration in the West emerged in the context of a mood of exhaustion with religious strife following the Reformation and a grudging acceptance of the reality of a morally plural world. In the mid-seventeenth century, when Locke, in the *Letter on Toleration*, tried to make this principle part of any legitimate political order, this mood was still dominant. Even Locke could not fully extricate himself from it, as evidenced by his unwillingness to extend tolerance to atheists.[19] With John Stuart Mill in the nineteenth century, the tolerance of diversity finally began to have some positive value.

Mill argues that diversity helps promote intellectual and moral progress. Now in one sense, this makes the value of tolerance instrumental; this, of course, is part of Mill's strategy of arguing only from "utility."[20] But the instrumental status is a curious one, because Mill's idea of progress is such that one would have a hard time arguing that it is occurring unless there were some diversity in a society, expressed in a struggle of opinions and ways of life. Here the notion of an instrument, or means, to achieve some end is peculiar, because one cannot really substitute any other such instrument. If the means is in this sense essential to the end, it becomes, as it were, part of the definition of the end. If this is true, Mill seems to have straddled an interesting issue. When tolerance is seen in the purely utilitarian way, Mill does not really disturb (although he does not actually endorse) the traditional attitude of considering tolerance as some-

19 John Locke, "Letter on Toleration," in *Locke on Politics, Religion and Education,* ed. by Maurice Cranston (New York: Macmillan, 1965), pp. 139–40.
20 John Stuart Mill, "On Liberty," in *On Liberty and Other Writings,* ed. by Stefan Collini (Cambridge: Cambridge University Press, 1989), p. 14.

thing we *must bear grudgingly* for the sake of something else; but when tolerance begins to have a value in itself, then we should in some sense *celebrate* or *delight in it.*[21]

If one asks Mill why we ought to celebrate diversity or difference, one answer would be that its presence in a society is a sign that we, as fallible creatures, are pursuing moral and intellectual truth in the only fashion we can. To celebrate diversity or difference is to celebrate the pursuit of truth. The underlying emphasis on fallibility is an important one for present concerns, because it begins to thematize finitude. And yet, I would suggest that Mill does not take us far enough here. When one makes fallibility the key issue, human being is still too one-sidedly tied to the responsibility to act. The metaphor of hunting, of pursuing the truth, subtly dominates the picture. A defender of Mill might immediately object here that there is another way of interpreting Mill, one that does not make truth and progress central. On this view, diversity and difference should be affirmed simply because they are essential components of a society that values "individuality": having each person make as many decisions for herself as possible, allowing each to draw upon and develop her own creative powers. If this interpretation is accepted, then celebrating individuality would seem to come fairly close to the idea of celebrating otherness. Perhaps this is so. But, as I noted in Chapter 2, there remains the deeply unsettling question of how someone with Mill's values and sensitivity could refer so cavalierly to the appropriateness of despotism for non-Western "barbarians."[22] If Mill's regard for difference, constructed solely with the resources of the liberal tradition, could stumble so badly, does it not seem reasonable to look for other resources that might embed in us a stronger propensity to hesitate in the face of such judgments?

It is at this point that the notion of finitude and the other

21 The idea of celebrating diversity might seem as traditionally American as apple pie. Diversity is extolled by American political leaders in practically every election. Without totally denigrating this phenomenon, one still has good reason for not taking it at face value, in the same way social scientists have learned that a large proportion of Americans who claim to support tolerance and civil liberties in general terms also express fairly intolerant attitudes when faced with concrete situations. For an overview of various studies on this topic, see Harry Holloway with John George, *Public Opinion: Coalitions, Elites and Masses,* 2nd ed. (New York: St. Martin's Press, 1986), pp. 66–71.

22 Mill, *On Liberty,* pp. 13–14, 20ff, and 56ff.

postmodern insights I have developed can be introduced. One does not neglect truth or individuality, but the mood of delight that supports diversity or difference has a new source intensifying that commitment. I have suggested in earlier chapters that, as the anchors of modern certainties increasingly lose their hold, finitude may come to be commemorated in ways that more immediately inform our everyday life. This new orientation will be tuned by a mood of grieving delight. I have already indicated how the dimension of grief might resensitize us to injustice. The dimension of delight likewise might manifest itself in a deepened concern for fostering difference. When we no longer define ourselves primarily in relation to a faith in God, or nature, or progress, the presencing of difference takes on a far different value. Now it is not in the first instance something to be accounted for, normalized, or grudgingly tolerated, but rather something to be celebrated. Attention to and delight in the presencing of difference is a primary way we become at home in homelessness, a way we sensitize ourselves to the sublime of everyday life. To care for difference becomes an affirmation of our finitude.

This reorientation does not promise something like an immaculate "politics of delight." Large, complex societies will always be heavily constructed around organizational routines and institutional projects, from the perspective of which the appearance of difference will often elicit more irritation than delight. The more the sway of the responsibility to act dominates a situation, the more this will be the case. The real issue is how to relax the pull of this responsibility before, within, and after such routines and projects; how to create slack and space within which the mood of delight can flourish. Part of this task will be to think creatively about when, where, and how intersubjective difference can be actively fostered.

It might be objected right off that in liberal democratic polities today there is really no necessity for such fostering. Rather than experiencing a paucity of new discourses, we are in fact awash in them. With a bit of cleverness, proponents of almost any kind of new discourse can catch the public's ear. In fact, one might even counter postmodern hyperbole by suggesting that something like the vision of the American artist Andy Warhol is increasingly descriptive of social reality: Anyone can become famous for fifteen minutes. In one sense such an objection has more than a bit of truth, but in another sense it is deeply misleading. Certainly there has been no period in history in which it is easier for a determined group to come to public attention through the mass media, primarily television. However, at the same time, it is necessary to realize how, in the United States especially, such emergence into public life is deeply and systematically structured. Actually, Warhol was overly generous in giving everyone fifteen minutes. It is rather the thirty-second sound bite and video clip that are ubiquitous. These constitute the dominant idiom of a televisual reality to which any discourse must conform.

The fact that such an idiom does not structure discourse in content-neutral ways has not been overlooked. Mainstream American political leaders, although frequently criticizing the media, learned in the 1980s how something they thought was a constraint to getting their message through was, in fact, a subtle ally. Clearly, one lesson of electoral politics during the Reagan and Bush years is that the short sound bite and video clip are the perfect idiom for reanimating dominant social myths, glorifying conformist values, and intensifying hostility to those who are coded as threatening others. It is not difficult to conclude that if the dominant idiom of televisual reality enhances the ease with which these sorts of messages are transmitted, then it is implicitly hostile to messages that depart from the mainstream.[23] The more different the message, the more difficult the hearing.

The point of suggesting this is not to claim the existence of a closed, one-dimensional televisual reality. Very little in an informationalizing society is so straightforward. Cable television and satellite dishes, as well as the increasing quality and decreasing cost of video equipment, all create possibilities for multiple idioms. The real question is, given such ambiguity, what should be the initial assumption upon which social and political theorists operate: that otherness pretty much gets adequate expression or that such expression is perpetually a problem? It is worth remembering here that self-congratulatory assumptions about the sufficiency of formal freedoms of speech, press, and association for the expression of grievances have caused acute embarrassment

23 See Timothy Luke's analysis of the interface between radical ecologists and the mass media in "Ecological Politics and the New Localism: Earth First! as an International Environmental Liberation Movement," paper presented to the International Sociological Association, Madrid, July 1990.

once before to sociologists and political scientists. In the 1950s and early 1960s, it was assumed by many interest group pluralists that any group with a substantial grievance would get an adequate hearing within government. The deceptiveness of that platitude was demonstrated again and again in the late 1960s and 1970s as urban violence, antiwar protests, and the women's movement erupted beyond the borders of the normal arenas of interest group struggle. Perhaps the long-term lesson to be learned is that one ought to operate on the alternative assumption that there are always social others out there who are not getting an adequate hearing. To think in a postmodern sense here would mean making this assumption without at the same time bringing along other strong assumptions traditionally made by radical critics about necessary forms and subjects of oppression, as well as about the character of the real interests of those who have not been adequately heard.[24]

In making the alternative assumption, one drops the simple image of a (different) voice speaking up, directly and clearly, to the ear of the public. Whether the voice speaks, how it speaks, and how it is heard all become more problematic. As noted in the last chapter, Nancy Fraser neatly thematizes this whole arena of issues with the concept of the "sociocultural means of interpretation and communication." These means include

> the officially recognized vocabularies in which one can press claims; the idioms available for interpreting and communicating one's needs; the established narrative conventions available for constructing the individual and collective histories which are constitutive of social identity; the paradigms of argumentation accepted as authoritative in adjudicating conflicting claims; the way in which various discourses constitute their respective subject matters as specific sorts of objects; the repertory of available rhetorical devices; the bodily and gestural dimensions of speech which are associated in a given society with authority and conviction.[25]

If one thinks of the problem of the emergence and expression of radically different discourses in this more complex way, and if

24 This does not mean that the topic of real interests should be completely dropped, however; see my *The Recent Work of Jürgen Habermas*, ch. 4.
25 Nancy Fraser, "Toward a Discourse Ethic of Solidarity," *Praxis International* 5 (January 1986), p. 425. Reprinted in *Unruly Practices: Power, Discourse and Gender in Contemporary Theory* (Minneapolis: University of Minnesota Press, 1989).

one is concerned not just with tolerating but also with fostering such otherness, then one has already projected a distinctive agenda for both empirical investigation and normative analysis. There is initially the question of simply trying to understand how the various components of these means of interpretation and communication function. Then there are two immensely complex questions with both normative and empirical dimensions: Which of these components function in ways that disempower or fail to empower significant segments of society? And what sorts of changes in the control of these means might begin to bring improvement? In regard to the second question, the complexity becomes quite apparent if one contrasts this problem with the traditional Marxian one. In broad terms anyway, Marxists were quite clear about what "control" of the means of production meant. But there is no simple change of control that will, for example, transform the "paradigms of argumentation accepted as authoritative in adjudicating competing claims." One could, of course, attempt something of this sort within a totalitarian framework, but that would clearly violate values deeply embedded in postmodern thinking. Thus the issue of restructuring the sociocultural means of interpretation so that other discourses are fostered or empowered can probably be approached only in piecemeal, experimental ways that apply to everything from primary school curricula to the ownership and access structure of mass media. In the present context, my task is not to speculate about the specific shape of such changes, but rather to suggest that if one shifts from endorsing only tolerance to endorsing tolerance and fostering, then one shifts the burden of proof in regard to important institutions and media. They must now justify their present structure in the face of criteria more demanding than traditional liberal ones.

B

The preceding discussion has attempted to show the need to put the notion of fostering otherness into the heart of political thinking. I want to tighten the focus now and try to make some progress toward a conception of justice that is more sensitive to such fostering. In this subsection, I ask how a new pluralist account differentiates between forms of otherness; when they are to be fostered and when they are to be constrained. In the next subsection, I examine more closely the idea of a state that does such fostering.

The issue of constraint on plurality is opened up in Lyotard's account of justice. As with other postmoderns, his initial difficulty in regard to justice is how to defend principles – however minimal – necessary to provide some normative guidance to ethical–political life without thereby generating some illegitimate closure to otherness. Lyotard's efforts are noteworthy because other postmoderns have a tendency to shy away from this difficulty, preferring the comparative safety of simply extolling otherness and denouncing modern society. But without the kind of account Lyotard tries to give, postmodern political reflection ends up generating only guidelines and speculations about "strategies for survival" in contemporary society, with no apparent normative responsibility on the part of any given strategy to any other.[26] No postmodern thinkers I know of would give blanket endorsement to the explosions of violence associated with, say, the resurgence of ethnic group nationalism in the Soviet Union or with the growth of street gangs in Los Angeles. And yet it is not at all clear that they have a normative discourse available to condemn such violence.[27] At some point, one must have a way of arguing that not all manifestations of otherness should be fostered; some ought to be constrained.

The issue of constraint can be disaggregated onto two levels. First, there must be some global principle of pluralism, giving it a basic normative shape. And, second, there must be some more specific procedural principles providing further normative guidelines for situations where plural forms of life come into conflict.

Lyotard recommends the following global principle of pluralist justice: "One must maximize as much as possible the multiplication of small narratives."[28] Although Lyotard does not explore the implications of this principle to any substantial extent, it does appear to imply some constraint. First, the principle might be

26 Frederic Jameson incorrectly lumps Lyotard together with other poststructuralists who seek only to elucidate some strategy for "surviving under capitalism" ("Forward" to Lyotard, *The Postmodern Condition*, p. xviii). This seems to me to overlook the clear implications of *Just Gaming*, originally published in the same year as *The Postmodern Condition*.

27 Having the resources to give a principled condemnation of this violence does not, of course, preclude a simultaneous condemnation of injustices in the society as a whole that may help explain the occurrence of such violence.

28 Lyotard and Thébaud, *Just Gaming*, pp. 59, 87.

taken to mean that master narratives or metanarratives are fair targets for suppression. I doubt if Lyotard intends this. Probably he only wants to say that such narratives will take care of themselves; only small ones need fostering. But that still requires someone to be continually in the business of separating metanarratives from all the others. This hardly seems to be an enterprise likely to have much legitimacy unless one were to rely on a fairly standard liberal criterion: Groups that adhere to some metanarrative *and* use it to justify the suppression of others can be prohibited from such action. But surely this constraint would apply to behavior associated with any sort of narrative.

I think that Lyotard does indeed want to foster a radical proliferation of all sorts of narratives but, at the same time, to attach a broad prohibition on certain sorts of action that might claim justification from a given narrative. Such a prohibition cannot be inferred directly from the principle itself, but his intention becomes clear in the supporting discussion. There he draws upon classical Greek philosophy. The attempt of one narrative, no matter of what kind, to dominate another is condemned by Lyotard as *pleonexia* or excess, as opposed to proper order, or balance. But *pleonexia* had significance in Greek philosophy primarily in relation to a theory of the virtues that specified certain substantive ideals of individual character.[29] When Lyotard uses the concept, however, it has a kind of deus ex machina character: Suddenly, the affirmation of radical or excessive proliferation is chastened by an ideal of balance that condemns excess. Lyotard's heart may be in the right place here, but the problem remains that he has not yet given a coherent account of the different components of his principle of plurality.

Given the care with which Walzer elaborates his account of justice, one might expect that he would provide a more illuminating explication of an overall principle of plurality. In his account, this principle is what transforms the carefully elaborated thesis about the distinctiveness of meanings in different social spheres into a normative claim about the rightness of protecting the autonomy of distinctive spheres. The principle itself takes something like the following form: One ought to recognize and respect the cultural creations of others.[30] What is surprising is that in a book

29 See Plato, *The Republic*, 586b.
30 Walzer, *Spheres of Justice*, pp. xii, 314.

that mounts such a massive assault on moral universalism, so little is said about this principle that is accorded universal validity.[31]

This unsatisfactory state of affairs in regard to a global principle within new pluralist accounts of justice is to be found again in the way the problem of constraint is conceptualized on a more concrete level. The reason the latter is significant is that a global prescription to respect and foster diversity provides little guidance in specific situations in which different spheres or forms of life come into conflict. When such conflict actually arises, one needs more direct normative guidance. In such cases, Walzer correctly suggests that justice "requires that the society be faithful to the disagreements, providing institutional channels for their expression, adjudicative mechanisms, and alternative distributions."[32] This all seems very reasonable but also extraordinarily vague in terms of any normative guidelines from the perspective of which disagreement is to be handled. The general principle of respect for others provides some normative direction, but hardly enough to warrant much confidence in the expectation that the various procedures Walzer mentions will result in some defensible mix of constraint and fostering.

As I emphasized at the beginning of the chapter, new pluralist accounts are deeply suspicious of the sorts of universalist, determinate principles of justice that provide quick resolution of the constraint problem. This suspicion is shared with communitarian critics of a theory like Rawls's. Communitarians themselves, however, have little difficulty with constraint. Legitimate constraints on plurality have their source in a community's traditions.[33] This route, however, is not attractive to most postmoderns. Although they tend to stress the embeddedness of individuals – in bodies, groups, discourses, language games, and so on – they are highly resistant to resolving the big normative questions through a straightforward appeal to the authority of tradition.[34] And

31 Ibid., pp. 17–20. Walzer has recently confronted the problem of universalism in "Two Kinds of Universalism," paper presented to a conference on "Deconstruction and the Possibility of Justice" at the Cardozo School of Law, New York City, November 1989.

32 Ibid., p. 313.

33 See especially MacIntyre, *After Virtue*; and *Whose Justice? Which Rationality* (Notre Dame, Ind.: University of Notre Dame Press, 1988).

34 Richard Rorty, whom some would classify as a postmodern thinker, does accept such a straightforward appeal to *our* tradition; see "Habermas and Lyotard on Postmodernity," in *Habermas and Modernity*, ed. by Richard Bernstein (Cambridge, Mass.: MIT Press, 1985), p. 166.

Walzer, for all his apparent communitarian sympathies, shares this resistance, even if his rationale is not so clear in *Spheres of Justice*.

If Walzer and Lyotard thus share a resistance to determinate principles as well as to the monolithic authority of tradition, then the question of the source of specific constraints on plurality is still not answered. Walzer's book, as I indicated, basically leaves us in the dark here. Lyotard, however, stakes out a distinctive position. Constraint for him can come only in the form of free, flexible, contractual arrangements.[35] Presumably, he thinks that such arrangements will, within the horizon of multiplicity, provide the most just way of managing conflicts, since they operate to maintain maximum freedom for diverse forms of life. In effect, contract provides the only acceptable form of "passage" over the abyss of heterogeneity (see the discussion on pp. 87–8 of Chapter 5).

Lyotard is not particularly comfortable with this resolution of the problem. Contract can be endorsed only in the sense that it is the least objectionable alternative; it minimizes the "wrongs" in a heterogeneous world. And, as Lyotard says, the best we can aim for is a politics of "lesser evil." By "evil" he means "the incessant interdiction of possible phrases, a defiance of the occurrence, the contempt of Being." But even after this lowering of expectations, Lyotard remains a bit ambivalent about his endorsement of contract. He suggests rather vaguely that this mode of managing heterogeneity might align itself far too comfortably with the imperatives of societal rationalization.[36]

Had Lyotard reflected further on his own misgivings, he might have had even more serious doubts about his unqualified endorsement of contractual arrangements. At this level of normative analysis, such endorsement generates a thorough blindness to the structural inequalities that are reproduced in processes of societal rationalization.[37] The freedom of participants in contractual negotiations is always problematic until one has

---

35 Lyotard, *The Postmodern Condition*, p. 66.
36 Lyotard, *The Differend: Phrases in Dispute*, trans. by George Van Den Abbeele (Minneapolis: University of Minnesota Press, 1988), pp. 140, 149; and *The Postmodern Condition*, p. 66.
37 See my "Habermas' Communicative Ethics and the Development of Moral Consciousness," *Philosophy and Social Criticism* 10 (Fall 1984), pp. 41–2; and Seyla Benhabib, "Epistemologies of Postmodernism: A Rejoinder to Jean-François Lyotard," *New German Critique* 33 (Fall 1984), p. 124.

evaluated the degree of inequality existing between the participants. Otherwise one blindly endorses even the Hobbesian contract in which the first party "freely" agrees to give up his wallet
in return for the second party's agreeing not to shoot him. Another related problem is the advantage a pure reliance on contract would appear to give to groups that are strongly benefited
by the status quo. Any proposed change in the status quo could
be effectively vetoed by them.

The foregoing overview of constraint, both in a global and in a
specific sense, leads to the conclusion that new pluralist accounts
of justice are not in the best of shape in relation to this issue. Once
again, I would argue that the two senses of responsibility, interpreted as I have suggested, provide a perspective that could help
alleviate the difficulty. As was shown, Lyotard's global principle of
pluralism is stated in such a way that the problem of constraining
certain manifestations of otherness can be solved only by grasping
a principle (avoiding *pleonexia*) whose foreignness to Lyotard's
other postmodern concerns is startling. Alternatively, Walzer's
global principle of respect for the cultural creations of others
clearly orients us toward constraint, but he seems surprisingly
uninterested in providing arguments in terms of which this principle is to recommend itself to us. Moreover, respect for others does
not clearly entail the orientation to fostering that would be necessary in order to address adequately the full range of postmodern
concerns.[38]

When the global question of a principle of plurality is re-
phrased in terms of a sense of responsibility to otherness, and
when the proper way to answer that sense is construed in the
intersubjective sphere as a commitment to a lightness of care,
then the beginnings of a somewhat more satisfactory orientation
to fostering and constraint emerge. The mood and measure of
such a lightness of care would, first, sustain a commitment
toward fostering otherness, born of a deeper understanding of
finitude and the delight in difference emerging therefrom. Cor-
respondingly, it would also sustain a commitment to constraint,
since the urge to dominate constitutes a refusal to bear witness
to one's limits, a refusal to recognize finitude. Actions that
dominate or systematically manifest a failure to respect others

---

38 In a moment I will show how Walzer, in an essay written after *Spheres of Justice*,
tries to accommodate the value of fostering; but I will also show why that
attempt is flawed.

are a willful forgetting of an inescapable dimension of human being.

The resources for more specific guidance on constraining plurality, however, will not emerge from reflection upon what it means to answer the sense of responsibility to otherness. Such reflection can at most clarify an underlying sensibility with which we should engage others. More specific normative guidance for permitting and constraining courses of action must come from reflection responding more directly to the sense of responsibility to act and manifesting itself in rules for adjudicating claims among actors. I have suggested repeatedly the value of Habermas's communicative ethics. Now one can see exactly where it fits and why it is appropriate. Like Walzer and Lyotard, Habermas wants to move away from the idea of universally valid, substantive principles of justice. His alternative is a universalist, discursive, procedural approach. He argues that there are certain universally valid procedural constraints implicit in our very idea of what coming to a rational agreement means. In disputes, these procedural principles legitimately constrain our arguments about the justness of a given norm.[39]

Lyotard and Walzer are both deeply suspicious of this project. I argue, though, that these suspicions are not well founded and that communicative ethics is a necessary component of a plausible, radical pluralist view. What bothers Lyotard and Walzer is their conviction that Habermas's perspective has embedded within it an imperative requiring us to flatten out differences on the way to the goal of a rational consensus on legitimate norms. Essentially we have nothing more than a great engine of homogenization, driving forward under the banner of universal reason and progress.[40] Interpreted in this way, communicative ethics would seem anything but useful for present concerns. But such an interpretation borders on caricature. What Habermas argues is only that there is an obligation, implicit in linguistic interaction, to justify the norms one proposes to others. The dialogical machinery of argumentation is not like the logic of markets and bureaucracies

---

39 For a summary of Habermas's arguments, see my *The Recent Work of Jürgen Habermas,* chs. 3 and 4.

40 Walzer claims that Habermas's model of normative discourse is intended "to press the speakers toward a preordained harmony"; "A Critique of Philosophical Conversation," *The Philosophical Forum* XXI (Fall–Winter 1989–90), p. 186. See Lyotard, *The Postmodern Condition,* pp. 65–6.

(to which postmodern thinkers seem to want to connect it); it makes little sense to understand discourse as an imperative arbitrarily invading new domains of social life. Rather, this machinery is engaged only when actual disagreement in some domain emerges, and the participants' intuitive knowledge of the procedural criteria of argumentation merely acts as an always imperfectly realized, regulative ideal. As I noted in Chapter 5, even Derrida cannot do without some similar notion of a normative obligation implied when actors take up a dialogue; and Foucault, in a late interview, also spoke in this vein.[41] In Habermas, this obligation is explicated in detail. His claim is that the know-how of rational justification is part of the communicative competence of individuals in modern societies. When normative conflicts arise, antagonists, insofar as they commit themselves to reason, know that a just outcome can emerge only if the norms proposed are ones to which all who are affected by them can agree.[42]

But critics are also concerned that Habermas's idealized reconstruction of our intuitive sense of rational, normative argumentation elevates theorists or philosophers to a position of illegitimate authority over ordinary citizens. The former become arbiters of the "correct" interpretation of our own intuitions and how well we follow the rules of practical discourse in a given dispute. However, this concern is also unwarranted. In communicative ethics, there is no expertise that can give one ultimate authority to say flatly that some substantive outcome of an actual discourse is just or unjust. The theorist can project the hypothetical course of a discourse – something that involves the risky imputation of arguments and interests to participants – but this construction does not have any special claim to validity. Or the theorist can observe the outcome of an actual discourse and criticize it on the basis of ways in which she judges it to depart from communicative rationality. Again, this judgment has no special validity. It merely provides a basis for citizens possibly rethinking the outcome, or a basis for investigating things like possible systematic biases in that discourse. In sum, nothing in communicative ethics allows the expert to place herself in a position of final authority versus the actual argumentation of real people.

41 Foucault, "Polemics, Politics and Problematizations: An Interview," in Paul Rabinow, ed., *The Foucault Reader* (New York: Pantheon, 1984), pp. 382–3.
42 See the summary of Habermas's position in my *The Recent Work of Jürgen Habermas*, ch. 4.

If the critics' suspicions about communicative ethics are thus largely misplaced, there does remain a sense in which some suspicion still appears warranted. The minimal procedural criteria of justice are part of the intuitive knowledge of *modern* speakers; and this does indeed imply some sort of metanarrative about reason and modernity.[43] Habermas's notion of normative justification is part of the culture of modernity and is deeply implicated in the tradition of liberalism. Although a critic like Lyotard may misleadingly overemphasize the tendency of Habermas's project to flatten out otherness, it is nevertheless undeniable that its supporting metanarrative privileges some things and marginalizes others.

It is undoubtedly the case that Habermas has sometimes not been sufficiently sensitive to the blindness generated by his metanarrative of modernity. But for present purposes, I am considering communicative ethics and its associated metanarrative of reason and progress *within* a broader framework that continually calls attention to this sort of conceptual blindness. The general orientation to radical pluralism should, as I have shown, be constituted as a way of answering the sense of responsibility to others. And the sensibility that animates that orientation is what is to be relied upon to foster an awareness of the limits that a perspective like Habermas's, by itself, cannot perceive. If this is so, then perhaps the problem that emerges at the metanarrative level can be grappled with in a somewhat different light. Too often, postmodern thinkers proceed as if unconditional victory over a modernist opponent is achieved as soon as that opponent's metanarrative is exposed. But things are not so simple.

First of all, it seems likely that one cannot discuss justice and collective action in any sustained fashion without implying at least some elements of a metanarrative. As critics have pointed out, Lyotard himself is entangled in a metanarrative about modernity.[44] And my notion of the two senses of responsibility certainly implies a story about the learning and unlearning that modernity has engendered. But the story has no foundation in a traditional philosophical sense. It simply offers itself as a candi-

---

43 Habermas, "Reply to Critics," in John B. Thompson and David Held, eds., *Habermas: Critical Debates* (Cambridge, Mass.: MIT Press, 1982), p. 253.

44 Douglas Kellner, "Postmodernism as Social Theory: Some Challenges and Problems," Special Issue on Postmodernism of *Theory, Culture and Society* 5 (June 1988), pp. 252–3.

date for the position of the most satisfactory general interpretation of modern individuality and social life. And "satisfactory" here means only that it is affirmed upon reflection as usefully addressing the needs, frustrations, dissatisfactions, and sense of achievement modern actors feel.

Taking all this into account, one can assess Habermas's metanarrative in a way that is different from his own evaluation, as well as from that of his postmodern critics. First, taken within the overall perspective I am offering, that metanarrative can be seen as telling only one part of a larger story about modernity.[45] Moreover, it can be interpreted in a more clearly pragmatic way, eliminating once and for all any lingering suspicions that it necessarily entails some sort of foundationalist bottom line (even if Habermas himself sometimes implies this).

The pragmatic link between Habermas's metanarrative of reason and progress and the minimal, procedural criteria of justice offered by communicative ethics can be envisioned as follows. Normative disputes, in regard to which we wish to have some specific principles of justice, can be resolved in various ways. The participants might simply agree to stay as far apart as possible, or they might resort to force. But if they stick with the idea of persuading each other through speech, then they must let some

---

45 Habermas's metanarrative tells about the gains of modernity, but its accounting of losses does not cut deeply enough into the confidence of modernity. This point can be illustrated here in a specific way regarding the problems of plurality and justice. I have tried to defend Habermas's discursive scheme for deriving constraints on plurality in normative disagreements. It is not nearly as hostile to otherness as critics contend. Nevertheless, the lack of an adequate conceptualization of finitude makes one uneasy about how the issue of otherness is handled at certain points. Like Mill's, Habermas's notion of practical reason is strongly tied to the idea of fallibility in the hunt for just norms. One must hunt cautiously and hesitantly, listen to others, put oneself in their place, and so on. But, in the final analysis, these things remain guidelines for hunting, and they can get forgotten in the bustle of a particular chase. When, on the contrary, one identifies a responsibility to otherness at as deep a philosophical level as the responsibility to act, there is a stronger independence to the moods and attitudes associated with hesitation and listening to the other. One cannot speak with certainty about exactly how this difference would affect the outcome of any particular normative dispute. An orientation toward both senses of responsibility cannot guarantee the identification of $X + 1$ dimensions of otherness, whereas Habermas's would identify only X. But this kind of indeterminacy in specific cases does not matter all that much. My primary concern is with broad areas of thematization. A more independent attention to phenomena of injustice and to the whole issue of fostering are all that I would claim emerge out of a sensitivity to the responsibility to otherness that is greater than that of Habermas's communicative ethics.

criteria of practical, normative reason guide their discourse.[46] And yet, what if disagreement breaks out at the level of these criteria? One cannot tackle this problem very satisfactorily with a discourse about the criteria of discourse. The attempt at justification has to move to the narrative dimension.[47] If one is persistently pressed to say why the criteria of normative justification ought to be understood in a certain way, one is forced to contextualize that judgment progressively up to the most general and comprehensive level of narrative about one's culture. And at this level, what we have is not simply another, slightly bigger, narrative than all the others floating around in our culture. Rather, we have a narrative that is recounted to those with whom we radically disagree, with the intention of showing them that they could freely recognize themselves as having a place within it, could find some sense of affirmation within it.

If Habermas's metanarrative is understood in this fashion, then it is worthy of being rescued from the ash can of history into which postmoderns have confidently tossed it. His complex and sophisticated story about the rational potential of cultural modernity – a central part of which is his ideal of normative discourse – and the tension in which it stands to the actual course of societal rationalization or modernization has much to recommend it. It is a self-critical metanarrative of the learning that has taken place in the modern world. And the conception of communicative ethics that it supports should, accordingly, be understood as a persuasive source for the sorts of specific normative guidelines that a new pluralist conception of justice requires.

C

I have shown why the theme of fostering otherness is important and why, when it is embedded in a perspective encompassing two senses of responsibility, it does not have to end up implying

---

46 I use the phrase "practical, normative reason" merely to indicate a dispute whose settlement requires some agreement on criteria that goes beyond simple bargaining. Of course, such bargaining may resolve the dispute and thus preempt the necessity for further reflection on criteria of normative argumentation.

47 The shift from a language of specific claims and practical argumentation about them to a language of narrative reflects the fact that, at a certain level of discourse, one is less testing arguments for rightness than asking oneself whether a given narrative offers a plausible practical context for one's life.

that "anything goes" normatively. I want to turn finally to the more direct institutional question of how the sphere of activity of the liberal state ought to be rethought if it is to engage in this fostering.

Lyotard is of little help here. His remedy of contractual arrangements seems largely designed to keep the state's role as minimal as possible. Nor is Walzer, in *Spheres of Justice*, very helpful. One has the feeling that the state should help preserve and maintain *existing* groups, subcultures, and their "spheres" of meanings, but this is not made very clear; nor does he indicate that the state might have a more affirmative role to play in actively fostering newly *emerging* spheres of social meaning.

More recently, however, Walzer has addressed these issues in a direct way. In a remarkable essay, he sketches a justification for a state that, on the one hand, violates the traditional liberal principle of neutrality toward social groups and yet, on the other hand, is not identical to the straightforward communitarian view that the state must promote some strong sense of community and the common good.[48] This sketch approximates the kind of conceptualization of the state that would emerge from the perspective I have developed, at least in the specification that the relevant terrain lies between liberalism and communitarianism. But the notion of a lightness of care and a sensitivity to the postmodern problematic would require certain modifications of Walzer's sketch. More specifically, Walzer inadequately analyzes the threat in relation to which this new sort of state activity is initiated. Further, his overall understanding of what might motivate broad public support for this redirection of politics has an unsatisfactory thinness about it.

For Walzer, the problem with the liberal state that enforces a neutral order of tolerance for all groups is that it is blind to certain "dissociative" forces in a liberal society. These forces that enervate our associative energies and sense of efficacy are traced to the liberal passion for mobility: geographic, social, marital, and political. The dilemma is that "the Four Mobilities represent," on the one hand, "the enactment of liberty and the pursuit of (private or personal) happiness"; but they also have the effect, on the other hand, of corroding the very "center" of

48 Walzer, "The Communitarian Critique of Liberalism," *Political Theory* 18 (February 1990), pp. 6–23.

the liberal tradition: the presence of healthy, plural, voluntary associations.[49]

What sharply distinguishes Walzer's analysis here from similar communitarian ones is his assertion that we (citizens of industrialized, Western societies) are indeed embedded, situated selves, but that what we are largely embedded in is a *liberal* tradition, not some "*Gemeinschaft* tradition . . . of the preliberal past." When the problem is framed this way, it can be resolved neither by a neutral state nor by a nonneutral, communitarian one seeking to stem dissociation by tightening the bonds of an antiliberal community. Rather, we must look to the ideal of a "deliberately nonneutral," liberal state that commits itself to maintaining a balance of values within its own tradition: a state that "fosters associative activities." Such a state has an obligation to "endorse and sponsor" groups when they are likely "to provide shapes and purposes congenial to the shared values" of the liberal tradition: "voluntary association, pluralism, toleration, separation, privacy, free speech, career open to talents and so on." If I read Walzer correctly here, this is a strong mandate to foster difference in society, limited only by something like the kinds of constraints that I discussed in Subsection B. Walzer's positive prescription is quite emphatic: The state is now in the business of "communal invention"; it should "always [be] on the look-out" for citizens who are willing to take greater responsibility for the life of their communities.[50]

Given the bold language incorporated in this political vision, there is a surprising asymmetry in Walzer's comprehension of the primary threat to it. Basically, it is only the effects of the Four Mobilities that are at issue. For someone as concerned with empowering and fostering, it would seem reasonable to understand these mobilities as intertwined with broader processes of societal rationalization and informationalization. If the threat is thematized more broadly, the problem of fostering is also broadened.

Two of the examples Walzer gives of fostering activity by the state are the support for the formation of labor unions in the 1930s in the United States and the allowance of tax exemptions and grants to enable religious groups to provide various forms

49 Ibid., pp. 11–12, 21. On Walzer's understanding, voluntary associations include groups that we are born into; the "voluntary" quality has to do with the freedom to leave a group.
50 Ibid., pp. 14, 16–17, 20.

of welfare services. Now there is nothing wrong with these examples per se. Presumably, part of Walzer's point in choosing them is to show that such fostering activity is already embedded in our political history. However, if one asks how we go on from here, the areas of potential fostering will likely be substantially expanded if we attend more directly to contemporary problems of informationalization and the subtle hegemony of some cultural patterns over others. And even without thematizing these phenomena, a broader attention to the problem of societal rationalization in general might lead one to additional arguments in support of some of the other initiatives Walzer wants to endorse. In regard to sustaining "communities of work and residence," Walzer applauds the recent passage of laws cushioning them from the effects of unilateral decisions by corporations to close factories.[51] But such cushioning hardly seems an adequate long-term response to the imperial logic of corporate capitalist markets if one is really interested in empowering and fostering. A more adequate response would be to think in terms of using public resources to enable decentralized, democratically controlled economic enterprises. Now Walzer has in fact argued for such institutions in the past, but he has stated his case purely on the grounds that the control of people within economic enterprises should follow the same principles we accept for the control of people within polities. In short, the prerogatives of property ownership do not extend as far as is commonly assumed. This argument, made also by Robert Dahl, is an important and valid one; and it may gain greater currency as the cold war increasingly fades away.[52] Nevertheless, such rethinking of property rights can be usefully supplemented by arguments from a

51 Ibid., p. 18. Walzer does seem somewhat concerned about the broader threat to which I am referring. In a footnote, he expresses the hope that his nonneutral state will "counteract the new inequalities of the liberal market and the bureaucratic state" (p. 23, n. 21).

52 Walzer, *Spheres of Justice*, pp. 291–203. See Robert Dahl, *A Preface to Economic Democracy* (New Haven, Conn.: Yale University Press, 1984). I suggest that such arguments might gain more currency in the near future because they are now less likely to be abruptly (and bogusly) discredited through a guilt-by-association maneuver: Any notion of economic democracy was previously tainted by association with regimes of the Soviet bloc. As these regimes pass away, so does a key trump card for proponents of the current structure of corporate capitalism. In the short term, of course, these proponents are basking in self-congratulations at having been vindicated on the stage of world history.

more explicitly postmodern direction. From this perspective, decentralized, democratically controlled enterprises offer a promising way of responding to the threshold problem discussed earlier. Such enterprises might be enabled or fostered by state power, but they would function in a broadly market-oriented society and thus would not be subject to the imperatives of state bureaucratic logic, as were all the experiments in Eastern Europe. But they would also, at least potentially, constitute a significant site of resistance to the smooth unfolding of the logic of corporate capitalism. This *resistance* would share nothing with the utopian Marxian notion of a total *elimination* of the logic of markets. The key point would be that this logic would be brought down to a level where it would be in continual and enhanced struggle with other logics emerging out of the life-world concerns of the communities in which those enterprises and their employees find themselves. Taken out of the corporate boardroom, decisions about things like profit and productivity would take place in a forum in which it is at least plausible to expect that factors like environmental and health damage, as well as obligation to the local community, might be given heavier weight.[53]

Like any specific institutional proposal claiming to foster otherness, decentralized, democratically controlled enterprises would generate their own forms of otherness and be open to critique in those terms. But an awareness of the perpetual necessity for remaining sensitive to otherness should not paralyze us before the choice of concrete institutional alternatives and the judgment of one as more defensible than another.

Finally, returning to Walzer's overall conceptualization of the nonneutral state, there is a second asymmetry that could also be remedied by placing it within the framework I have developed. The affective counterpart of the dissociative tendencies he seeks to stem is a deep sense of loss, of homelessness in our lives. Walzer's remedy for this loss is, to repeat, not the communitarian one of a warm hearth of *Gemeinschaft* and a broth of traditionalist tradition. His prescription is that we try to pay more attention to

---

53 For arguments that are similar, but advanced in different theoretical contexts, see Dahl, *A Preface to Economic Democracy*, pp. 100–1; and Claus Offe and Helmut Wiesenthal, "Two Logics of Collective Action," in Offe, *Disorganized Capitalism: Contemporary Transformations of Work and Politics* (Cambridge, Mass.: MIT Press, 1985), pp. 175ff.

the "intimations of community" within the constellation of liberal values. Although Walzer is right here about denying us a warm hearth, it is difficult not to feel that his alternative is to offer us a broth that, by itself, is just too thin. We should indeed pursue the echoes of community in the nontraditionalist tradition of liberalism.[54] But the sense of loss and homelessness probably needs to be addressed in terms of a more thoroughgoing realignment of modern consciousness. A remedy conceived at this level is, of course, no quick fix. There is only the slow process of learning to be at home in homelessness, of reorienting ourselves to our own finitude and the meaning of otherness. Without a rethinking of this magnitude, however, it seems to me that the kinds of new directions a more radical pluralism proposes will be unlikely to become embedded deeply enough in people's everyday lives. It has been the purpose of this book to begin to clarify what might be involved in such a rethinking.

54 Habermas seeks comparable sustenance from, and faces comparable problems with, the notion of "solidarity" with an "ideal communication community"; "Justice and Solidarity: On the Discussion Concerning Stage 6," in Christopher Wren, ed., *The Moral Domain: Essays in the Ongoing Discussion between Philosophy and the Social Sciences* (Cambridge, Mass.: MIT Press, 1990), pp. 244–6.

8

CONCLUSION

In the Preface, when the two senses of responsibility and the corresponding views of language were introduced, I said that neither side of the two pairs should be absolutely privileged over against the other. Although that is the intention I have had throughout this book, it is clearly the case that the responsibility to act and the action-coordinating view of language have been softly, but persistently, favored to some degree over the responsibility to otherness and the world-disclosing view of language. This fact is likely to make my efforts immediately rather suspect in the eyes of strong defenders of postmodernism.

In my defense, I would simply say that no one can avoid some sort of granting of priority in a discourse about the modern and the postmodern. I have granted a certain priority to one side of the two pairs of distinctions because my interest is to engage certain traditional ethical–political questions. But the whole aim of the book has been to show the costs of allowing such a positioning on this one side to be frozen into a one-sidedness. To that end, I have tried continually to ask how one works back toward the other side, with its distinctive sets of attunements and sensitivities.

Heidegger and the contemporary French thinkers I criticize have found any such strategy to be in too close collaboration with modernity and its imperatives. From my perspective these suspicions are welcome; they are part of what I mean by maintaining a fruitful tension between both pairs of distinctions. I have tried, in turn, to maintain the tension in a different way by asking how well these thinkers work back from the side they have privileged. At their worst, they occlude this task. Heidegger is the arch offender. At their best, they struggle honestly with the task. Beneath the roar and confusion of the battles over postmodernism, this quality is recurrently evident in Foucault, Derrida, and Lyotard. That makes them worthy antagonists for anyone who is trying to bring the modern Western heritage of ethical–political thinking into an engagement with some of the more perplexing phenomena of contemporary life.

INDEX